BEA
TABL

M000013846

Photo Credits with citation: *The Jackson Sun*

Photo Credit with citation: *The Courier*

Photo Credits: Aspell

Editing Service: Shelley Mascia
https://www.facebook.com/
ShelleysEditingService

Book and Cover Design: Tammy Yosich

Zoe Grace Publishing, LLC
Jackson, TN

First originally published by Zoe Grace
Publishing, LLC
www.zoegracepublishing.com

ISBN: 978-1-7364079-1-2 (Paperback)

Printed in the United States of America

To Aspell:

Thank you for allowing me to be a part of the story for sixteen years now. Thank you for believing in me, challenging me, and supporting me.

This book is dedicated to all the excellent staff, board members, and the overwhelming community support: Jackson, West Tennessee, and the State. Without our community's support, it would be virtually impossible to do what we do every day for those who suffer from alcoholism, addiction, and co-occurring disorders.

To Our Clients:

You are loved. You are enough. You are strong. You can recover your life and all the beauty it holds. Never give up.

Sincerely,

Tammy Yosich

Tammy Yosich

PROLOGUE

On April 16, 2021, Harold L. Montgomery turned 90 years old. Mr. Montgomery grew up in Pulaski, Tennessee, located in Giles County. Montgomery attended Martin College after serving in the military. At Martin College he studied to become a minister. There, he met and married the love of his life, Rebecca. They were married for nearly fifty years, and had six children, until brain cancer separated Harold and Rebecca.

When Montgomery was seventeen, he joined the United States Airforce and served his country from 1948 to 1952. He joined the other newly enlisted at Shepherd's Field, where they flew to a base in Germany. Montgomery served during The Berlin Airlift, whose base always had four planes in the air or getting loaded with food, coal, and a little wine to be delivered.

During the first three months, Montgomery trained to become an engine mechanic and loved it. *"I could get greasy like you're supposed to be,"* recalls Montgomery. However, the Air Force told him he would become a weather observer. It was a position he did not like and did

Sgt. Harold L. Montgomery records weather data at the instrument shelter.   Photos by Lt. Robert Holt

Source: *The Courier* Friday, March 28, 1952

not want but learned quickly that what the Air Force told you to do, you did. Montgomery says of his military service, *"I wouldn't take anything for it,"* but jokes, *"I would have sold it pretty cheap."*

While stationed in Germany, Montgomery learned about German beer. *"I liked what it did. I was backward and bashful, but after some of that German ale, I wasn't near as bashful."*

In 1953, after the war, Montgomery enrolled at Martin College. During Montgomery's first night at Martin College, he realized how dangerously close he was leaning towards becoming a full-blown alcoholic. During orientation, leadership at the college told the student body that the one thing they will not tolerate on campus was students drinking alcohol. That night, Montgomery and a friend went to the Legion Hall and closed it down. *"The environment,"* said Montgomery, *"just turned me around. I realized I was on thin ice. That night was my last drink. At that point, I stopped, and it turned my life in a new direction; I didn't mean too."*

After the President of Lambuth College (now the University of Memphis) made a presentation at Martin College, speaking about the beauty of his campus with such passionate that Montgomery and his wife, Rebecca, made their way to Jackson (Madison County, West Tennessee) to finish their education.

After graduating from Lambuth College in 1957, Montgomery was asked to return to the Columbia district to continue his pastoral work. However, Montgomery had already become established within four churches in Hardin County, Tennessee. Montgomery earned a Master's in Divinity from Vanderbilt University in 1960 and became an ordained minister. Montgomery's mission would evolve into helping individuals through the disease of addiction and settle into a life of recovery.

During his time in Middle Tennessee, he worked in a parsonage in Hollow Rock for three years. During his tenure he met a man who suffered from severe alcoholism. "Johnny" was a brilliant, great man and Montgomery's neighbor at the parsonage. "Johnny" would help anyone he could, and when he was close to functional, he did. Montgomery could see the potential "Johnny" had, but he couldn't get over the drink. There wasn't much advancement in the way of treatment in the late '50s.

During the late '50s, Montgomery had gone to see Dr. Frank Moore, a local doctor, about a case of athlete's foot. They struck up a conversation about alcoholics and the devasting destruction they cast on their lives and the lives of their loved ones. *"I had a lot of respect for Dr. Moore. I could take folks down to the Jackson Clinic, and he would come out to the car and try to help them. He told me to keep bringing them,"* remembers Montgomery. Dr. Moore told Montgomery if he was going to help people through their battles with addiction, he needed to meet two "Bob's": Bob Cox and Bob Aspell. Cox ran a local grocery store where most of the staff were in recovery, and Montgomery would become a disciple of Bob Aspell.

Montgomery met Bob Aspell in the early '60s and was fascinated by the intelligent man. *"Make no bones about it, Aspell was a grateful recovering alcoholic,"* said Montgomery. Aspell would take Montgomery along on Twelve-Step calls. Early Twelve-Step calls were often the only immediate 'treatment' offered in the West Tennessee area. These calls consisted of a family/friend or even the alcoholic themselves reaching out for help. A sober member of Alcoholics Anonymous (AA) would answer the call by visiting the alcoholic and utilizing the same suggestions that got them sober, extending those to the current sufferer. On these calls, Montgomery witnessed more severe cases of alcoholism; perhaps worse off than "Johnny." On these calls, one found out quickly that these people needed help and did not like what they were doing but could not stop drinking independently.

When Tennessee Psychiatric Hospital and Institute located in Memphis, opened between 1961 and 1962, it offered an experimental alcohol and drug program. In 1979, the Tennessee General Assembly greenlit the Department of Public Health to develop programs to prevent and treat alcohol and other drug abuse. By this time, the Jackson Area Council on Alcoholism (JACOA) was already treating alcoholics and in November/1979, Aspell had begun doing the same.

Montgomery and Aspell developed a lifelong friendship. Aspell refused to give up on those who lost hope of ever becoming sober. Aspell truly loved helping these people. One might say it became an addiction for Aspell and Montgomery: the joy of seeing someone wake up, come out of the fog, and go on to live a life free from addiction. Montgomery saw Aspell as a unique person and became someone he would serve beside until Aspell passed away.

It was through Bob Aspell that Montgomery met Nancy Tuchfeld and Sam Bergel. *"A wonderful Jewish lady,"*

Montgomery described Tuchfeld, *"whose mother dictated that she get treatment for her alcoholism or become disinherited. Nancy went to treatment in North Carolina and returned with a visceral mission to help the alcoholic who suffers. It was a sad day when we heard Nancy was terminally ill. She was such a beautiful lady."*

Montgomery met Sam Bergel in 1964. Bergel was a new board member for the JACOA, where Montgomery was also a board member. Bergel was a businessman involved in numerous enterprises, but his main business was people. He hired people who needed the pay far above their ability to perform the duties. *"Perhaps Sam dealt with the pain of his own life by ministering to others who were hurting. He helped bear the burden of many. Sam's heart stopped beating on December 3, 1976, but the great love which that heart held for humanity will surely live on in all who knew him,"* Montgomery wrote of his friend.

After Aspell passed in 1975, Montgomery began the journey to becoming the sole Executive Director of JACOA. Charlie Gay, Sr. was a volunteer with the organization and would visit with Montgomery nearly every day in his office at the New Southern Hotel, located in downtown Jackson. Gay saw the chronic alcoholics through the office window and told Montgomery, *"Harold, them boys are going to die if something isn't done."* This motivated Charlie to start a halfway house. Of course, Charlie knew as much about a halfway house as Montgomery knew of airplanes, nothing. But Gay was dedicated to get the alcoholics off the streets help for their sufferings.

Gay started a halfway house in an old Victorian located at 331 North Highland Avenue – just a few blocks from where he and Montgomery witnessed the suffering from the window. One simply did not tell Charlie Gay that he couldn't do it. Gay leaned on the words of Bob Aspell, *"All you need for an AA group is people, the Big Book, and a pot of coffee."* That may have been all Gay provided in those early days but thankfully, it was all many of them needed.

Montgomery would serve as Executive Director for JACOA for nearly four years but a lifetime of service to the alcoholic and addict. *"Helping alcoholics and addicts was part of what I was supposed to do,"* said Montgomery. *"Folks around here calling me a hero, but I've never considered myself such a thing. I just liked the experience of seeing somebody get it together. I loved them where they were, and sometimes that meant deploying some tough love. I feel like it has been a privilege to serve. There were many nights I wasn't home with my wife and six kids, but I truly thought I was doing what I was being called to do. You can be selfish, I suppose, without knowing it.*

Perhaps, I had an addiction to people getting the message. I can hardly be considered a hero. Well, I tried – I really tried to spread the message."

Spread the message he did. A countless number of

Harold Montgomery on this 90th birthday surrounded by family and friends.

individuals are living a life of recovery because of Harold Montgomery's dedication, compassion, and legacy. Richard Barber, Executive Director of Aspell, was in treatment at JACOA during Montgomery's tenure in 1986. During an interview with Montgomery, he pointed to Barber and said, *"I remember when you were in treatment."*

Barber replied, *"Yes, sir, that was 34 years ago, and I hope you don't mind if I consider you a hero because that is what you have been in my life."*

Harold L. Montgomery is a hero. His willingness to spread the message through his ministry, his love for the alcoholic and addict, and his love and trust in God, whom he trusted to take him on this lifelong mission to reach out to the suffering has proved his heroism time and again.

INTRODUCTION

"Thy word is a lamp unto my feet and a light unto my path."
Psalms 119:105

In the 19th century, Lamplighters turned night into day. A staple of the urban Victorian streetscape, the nostalgic image is of a lone man, walking a darkening city street as dusk descended behind him, extending his staff to ignite each dark, cold lamp stem to life with a small flame. Lamplighters lit those posts for miles, in every direction, so all travelers would find a light for whatever path they may be traveling.

T.A.M.B. of Jackson, TN., Inc., also known as Aspell, was founded in 1979 as a non-profit 501(c)(3) organization. The federal government places nonprofits in two categories, secular and faith based; Aspell is categorized secular. However, with just one visit to our nearly five-acre campus and meeting our people, you will quickly discover there is nothing secular about us. God is at the forefront of every decision and every action.

Aspell offers the opportunity to experience the warm, unifying, beacon of hope to all who visit, work, or serve the organization. Since 1979, Aspell has provided hope and love from what started as a corner lot. A lot that once held a significant structure where those who suffered from the ravages of alcoholism sought refuge. It is our firm belief that whether a representative of Aspell or a visitor, you have felt Bob Aspell and Charlie Gay's light in some way. This light has been the driving force that keeps each of us here and fighting the good fight.

Each person touched by our campus can become a lamplighter, a keeper of the flame for those coming behind. Our passionate hope is that one step becomes two, and the seeds planted lead to twelve. With each step, a lamp is lit for those struggling to find their way.

Neru Gobin, TDMHSAS[1] Office of Housing and Homeless Services Director, stated that Aspell is a *"Beacon of Light."* Aspell's beacon has been created by numerous dedicated and compassionate individuals planting seeds of hope, love, and compassion in the darkest times. This seed is planted with the initial phone call seeking help, throughout the continuum of care, and beyond.

Like the clients we serve, Aspell has experienced moments of uncertainty, setbacks, and obstacles. However, Aspell has proven to overcome those challenges utilizing a simple formula: always keep God at the forefront of every decision, be patient when we are delayed by God's Will, and always placing the needs of our clients above all else. While the future looks bright for Aspell and we have strategic plans

---

[1] Tennessee Department of Mental Health and Substance Abuse Services

drawn out, we focus primarily on the twenty-fours we have been given to change people's lives.

Let us never forget the first lamplighter was Jesus.

"Then Jesus spoke to them again, saying, "I am the light of the world. He who follows Me shall not walk in darkness but have the light of life."
John 8:12

This is the story of five visionary lamplighters who created T.A.M.B. and a legacy that continues today.

CHAPTER ONE

ROBERT J. ASPELL
<u>T</u>uchfeld, <u>A</u>spell, <u>M</u>oore, <u>B</u>ergel

"Newcomers are likely not to know that name (Bob Aspell) or why it's important to Jackson, Tennessee. But for those of us who have been in Jackson a while, it is a name that will forever be associated with dedication to a cause, a dedication to helping others."
--- *The Jackson Sun* (Sunday, June 7, 1981)

Source: *The Jackson Sun*, March 2, 1959

Robert J. Aspell (Bob), was born on February 13, 1909 in Cleveland, Ohio, to James and Elizabeth Aspell. Bob Aspell was a second generation American, coming from Irish and Canadian grandparents. His father was a bookkeeper for a gas company and his mother, a housewife.

In 1942, Bob enlisted in the U.S. Army and worked his way up to the rank of Master Sergeant. In 1954, Aspell is said to have ridden on an Illinois-Central rail, crouched in a boxcar as a hobo. He is also said to have hitchhiked into Jackson; a washed-up hungry, drunk, and down on his luck newspaper reporter. A good Samaritan motorist deposited Bob at the doorstep of the Salvation Army, who then took in 'one more drunk' and fed, clothed, and provided rest for the worn-out traveler.

Despite how he arrived, Aspell himself describes his arrival as, *"The man who came to dinner and stayed five years."* We certainly know he stayed much longer than that.

Aspell sought help for his alcoholism at the Salvation Army, then located on Union Avenue. An organization that Bob would dedicate his life and passion to for ten years. Aspell started with overseeing the Salvation Army's homeless lodge shortly after arriving in 1954. Around 1956, Aspell – potentially giving credence to his career as a newspaper reporter – started a column in *The Jackson Sun* titled, *"Your Salvation Army."* He wrote this weekly column for about six months. Aspell went on to become a field representative for the Salvation Army before retiring in the early 1960s.

Bob was a great storyteller, and in 1959, he tells a story of a client who was just a constant grumbler. The client complained everyone was against him, cannot get a ride, employers did not keep him, needed a shave, and constantly disheveled. Meanwhile, another client, "Clarence" – after pacing for a half-an-hour, finally got up the courage to ask, *"Mr. Bob, could I trade a pair of shoes that are too small for a pair that is too big?"* Confused, Bob finally figured out that Clarence understood there to be only two sizes of shoes: too small or too big. Returning to the grumbler, Bob firmly told him that if three companies saw fit to dismiss him, then he should take an inventory of himself! Furthermore, no one was obligated to give him a ride, wash his clothes, or shave his face. Soon, the grumbler began to face the reality that the problem was himself.

In his column *"Your Salvation Army,"* Bob discussed his share of interesting clients. "Buck" was quickly discovered by the other residents as an outsider because he was wearing a nightshirt, something of a luxury for the homeless men. *"Old Timer,"* who continued to tell the others that he was "going home soon," although he meant to Chicago to collect a pension. He was found later near a train track in Trenton, having died in an unfortunate attempt to jump on the railway car or perhaps a heart attack. He discussed a family's twenty-cent donation, which caused great moral debate for Bob. A close-knit family was down on their luck with a 39' pick-up truck that needed a tire. The family was fed, provided a room for the night, and the next day the truck was fitted with a new tire, which was hard to come by in 1959. The wife asked what they owed for the services, and Aspell replied, *"you owe us nothing, we accepted the opportunity of helping travelers in trouble."* The husband and wife looked at each other wordlessly and the wife reached into her pocket and pulled out two dimes, handing them to Bob. Concluding this column, he asked the reader: *"What to do?"* – as accepting it may appear overly merciful, but to deny it might deny the family's self-respect.

Bob was questioned about taking up tainted collections outside a drinking establishment, to which he replied, *"The only taint on that money is that there taint enough of it."* He went on to say that he hoped his presence there would be a witness to his Lord and Savior.

Aspell was often seen shaking the tambourine for the Salvation Army collections, and a known speaker before civic clubs and other charity organizations. Bob was an avid laborer for the 'least of these.' He was overwhelmed by the Grace of God that he obsessively took to shining his light as bright and as far as he could to save the next lost soul. In 1962, Bob was promoted and transferred to the Tennessee-Kentucky Salvation Army headquarters, where he worked directly under Brigadier Walter Swyers, Commander of the Tenn.-Ky. Division.

In an interview, he said,

> *"I shall never forget these 100 months I've been in Jackson, and I shall always remember (without being proud, but not with shame) that I came in desperate need, discouraged, dirty, hungry, and without hope. I shall never forget that here I found a community which had made provision for such as I."*

I believe Bob would be proud of the campus we have created in his honor –a community that makes provisions every day for people just like Bob Aspell. It is impressive our campus reflects such a man who would not live to see it come to fruition; however, we suspect we may have had some guidance from the other side.

In an interview before leaving Jackson for Louisville, Kentucky, Bob reflected on how gratifying it had been to witness the growth of the meager Salvation Army facilities on Union Avenue to the fine plant they had on South Royal. He hoped that the new building would receive funding and declared

that not even a "bullwhip" could cause him to miss a "mortgage burning" ceremony. We wish he could see, now, how his dream for the Salvation Army has become a reality for us here at T.A.M.B. – Aspell, his name's sake.

In June of 1964, the Jackson Area Council on Alcoholism (JACOA) was established, and Bob was named Director with Mrs. Nancy Tuchfeld (chairman) and Bob Allison (vice-chair). Dr. Frank Moore, Tuchfeld, and Bob presented to the Health, Welfare, and Safety Council (HWS) with details of a new program on alcoholism, ultimately becoming JACOA, a nonprofit volunteer organization. Tuchfeld stated in 1964, the Board of Directors were mostly

non-alcoholics with about 15% being 'cured alcoholics."
Bob noted that this was the only public group that
addressed the public health problem of alcoholism. At the

Source: *The Jackson Sun*, Friday, June 5, 1964

time, they estimated around
1,700 alcoholics in the area,
with 6 out of 100 high
school students becoming
an alcoholic. Today's
statistics lend credibility to
this dated prediction; our
data shows the age of first
use to be around 11-15 years
old. "*The problem cannot be corrected by pushing it out of
sight or passing laws*," Bob wrote in 1964, "*the public must
be informed, children and young people must be taught,
and treatment and information centers are needed.*"

Tuchfeld, Moore, and Aspell advocated that
"*sometimes the greatest treatment is to the family*" so that
they can understand the patient and their disease. They
discussed medical attention for the alcoholic and a halfway
house instead of jail. In 1964, Bob stated they had 65 clients,
and several of them belonged to Alcoholics Anonymous.

Dr. Frank Moore died on November 5, 1964. Moore
served in the U.S. Army Air Corp until 1945, retiring as a
Colonel. At the time of his death, Dr. Moore was the

Medical Director for The Jackson Clinic since 1950. He served on several boards dedicated to easing the alcoholics suffering, including JACOA. As Harold Montgomery remembers, Dr. Moore dedicated his life and profession to help the suffering alcoholic and addict. He met the patient where they were – literally- often meeting with them in the vehicle in the clinic's parking lot. Dr. Moore ignored the stigma surrounding the addict, remaining steadfast in his higher calling to care for those who suffer, who are sick in mind, body, and spirit.

Nancy Tuchfeld died December 11, 1966, and was known as a calm, confident leader with fierce determination that aroused people's consciousness in Jackson on alcoholism. Treating the alcoholic is possible and produces morally, economically stable, and a life-affirming person living in recovery. Tuchfeld's own recovery inspired others because she lived a productive life, free of alcohol that she had battled.

In June of 1975, Bob Aspell retired from JACOA after eleven years of service and overall, twenty-one years of service to his fellow

Copyrighted Material

man. After gaining strength in his sobriety, he dedicated his life to helping others quit drinking through good deeds. He quickly learned in 1954 that good works are done one day at a time – be it dipping soup for the hungry, providing a bed for the weary, or sharing the Grace of God to the lost soul. Through his good deeds, he learned about

Source: *The Jackson Sun*, October 23, 1957

the strength of a community, he understood human nature, and he realized a lot about himself. He illuminated a guiding light for which others were able to light their way out of darkness.

Bob was recognized across Tennessee as a compassionate leader who inspired others. During his retirement ceremony, former U.S. Senator Bill Brock stated that Bob Aspell meant service, concern, love, and giving of yourself. The Mental Health Commission noted that it takes a special kind of person to love the downtrodden and the unfortunate, that Bob Aspell was a special kind of person. Former Jackson Mayor Bob Conger praised Bob as having established himself as an institution through compassion for others. John Wilder, the Lt. Gov. at the time, praised Bob for making an immense, widely known, contribution to society. Others across the state said it would take a great many to fill the shoes of Bob Aspell. What did Bob Aspell have to say for himself? Aspell humbly stated that his career had been *"21 wonderful years,"* and as far as his leadership with JACOA, *"I had not been the leader of the organization, but a listener, always for the small, still voice of God. As far as what JACOA represents, I can only claim to have done the best I could."*

Bob led JACOA to become a leading substance abuse treatment facility during the '60s. It is indeed astonishing that decades after his death, our Aspell – his namesake – has become a leading treatment center across the state of Tennessee as well. In June 1975, Bob said, *"I retire tonight, but I'll be waiting in the wings, watching, feeling proud as I see the child run, and leap, and bang its knee, and get up again."* He was speaking at the time of JACOA, but it reads like a poetic foreshadowing of our organization.

Robert (Bob) J. Aspell died of a heart attack on September 29, 1975, at 66 years old. He had been in the hospital a week after suffering his third heart attack in less than a year. He just kept going,

JACOA Founder Aspell Dies Of Heart Attack

Source: *The Jackson Sun*, Monday, September 29, 1975.

and when he reached the Pearly Gates, he had exhausted all his earthly talents.

While Bob had no children of his own, he has repeatedly referred to his work as his 'child' and was eager to see his endeavors prosper – not for himself but for those in need. Many have said Bob was the closest we might come to meeting a saint. He was guided by the noblest of human labor – selfless service. He was lovingly described as a vigorous man with a spark in his soul and a twinkling in his eyes with an active sense of humor. A worldly man who set his passion on a once small community, Jackson, which he credited for saving his life. He was a scholar, a journalist, and a salvager of human resources. His life's journey was passionately altruistic. As a builder of humankind, he brought together people, money, and resources to fashion into a thriving legacy geared to help those who suffer from addiction. Bob knew from firsthand experience that a night in the drunk tank would not cure an alcoholic. You must help him to find a reason to stay sober.

In 1957, Bob explained to a *Jackson Sun* reporter that through the Salvation Army, he was able to return the help he received by dedicating his life to helping homeless wanderers. If Bob were here today, we believe he would describe the dedicated Board and staff of Aspell, as he said in 1959, *"By your vigorous yet compassionate action, you have made provisions for the weak, the helpless, the young, the old, and the afflicted; I am proud."*

Bob Aspell, Nancy Tuchfeld, Sam Bergel, and Frank Moore were the flames by which Charlie Gay lit his own lamp of helping the suffering alcoholic and addict. On December 3, 1976, Sam Bergel, the last of the founding tetrad, died. Bergel was known for giving his whole life for others' benefit. Harold Montgomery wrote, *"Sam's heart stopped beating that day, but the great love which that heart held for mankind will surely live on in all who knew him."*

One of Bergel's joys was to accompany disabled children to the Shriner's Circus; he loved his children and grandchildren – he loved everybody's children. No North Pole elf worked harder or enjoyed their work more than Bergel as he headed up the Salvation Army's Christmas Shop. Sam loved everybody but perhaps had a particular affinity to those who suffered and a deep desire to ease, or even bear some of the burden, their pain. Bergel was known for hiring people with a far more need for a paycheck than an ability to do the job. It was all about giving people a chance. Sam had a knack for collecting what some might call 'junk,' but he referred to as 'junique,' repurposing unique items that others considered junk. Likewise, he was able to see the uniqueness and quality of people that many in society considered worthless.

Bob Aspell lived his life dedicated to others, helping the most vulnerable among us, to live a life filled with faith, strength, and hope. Bob borrowed the flame from those who helped guide him and Charlie Gay, Sr., lit his own lamppost from the loving flame of Bob Aspell. Gay and Aspell shared a lifelong friendship that began in the early 1960s.

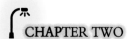

CHAPTER TWO

CHARLES EDWARD GAY, SR.

"I want to see a halfway house for alcoholic men in Jackson, Tennessee. I want the facility to be named T.A.M.B. in honor of Nancy Tuchfeld, Bob Aspell, Frank Moore, and Sam Bergel. These four individuals gave so much to create a program to deal with the great problem of alcoholism. "
---Charlie Gay, May/1979

"Local Half-Way House Urged for Alcoholics."

I *sincerely wish that all of you were aware that the alcoholic is a sick person on his way to physical, mental, and spiritual destruction.*

But alcoholism is a treatable sickness and many of us have been privileged to see broken, despairing men and women reclaimed and restored to a useful place in society.

I am a volunteer worker with the Jackson Area Council on Alcohol and Drug Abuse. I transport alcoholics to and from various treatment centers in Memphis and even in Tupelo, Mississippi. I have been greatly impressed with the effectiveness of what are called "half-way houses."

These facilities are non-medical treatment centers which effectively use recovering alcoholics as counselors. These half-way houses are effective in helping the alcoholic learn to be sober. And these facilities are operated on a low budget because they utilize non-medical and non-degreed staff. Many of these programs operate on $10 per day.

Rural West Tennessee very much needs such a half-way house and I want to see one in operation in Jackson to serve the needs of the alcoholic man who cannot afford hospital care.

I am retired and therefore have time to work at establishing such a half-way house. *I feel that to help establish such a facility and to see men broken by alcoholism restored to dignity and usefulness would be the greatest work of my life.*

I want to see a half-way house for alcoholic men in Jackson. I want the facility to be named T.A.M.B. in *honor of Tuchfeld, Aspell, Moore, and Bergel* who gave so much to create a program to deal with the great problem of alcoholism. I sincerely hope that many of you readers will share this dream.

This facility will have to be operated and proven to be beneficial to the community before it is funded by the state, United Way and Rehabilitation. This being the case, I implore you, the citizens of the Golden Circle, to support me in this project by sending in a generous donation to T.A.M.B. Box 2412.

This facility will house 11 to 20 men and will take quite a sum of money to open.

Give until it feels good. Contributions are deductible.

C. E. Gay Sr.

Source: The Jackson Sun, 2A Sunday, May 13, 1979 (bold/emphasis mine)

Charles Edward Gay, Sr. was born May 19, 1912, in

Okolona, Mississippi. Charlie was a retired engineer for the old *Gulf, Mobile, and Ohio Railway*. Charlie married Ruby M. Herndon on April 26, 1931, and at the time of Charlie's death, they had just celebrated their 52nd wedding anniversary. Charlie served as Aspell Manor's Program Director without pay because, as he frequently said, *"It's a labor of love, and I know what it's like."* Charlie Gay was certainly not afraid of a little labor for the dream he had for our campus in the late 1970s.

Having shared a lifelong friendship with Bob Aspell, it is no surprise that when Charlie Gay established a halfway house for alcoholic men in Jackson, he would name it after his friend and mentor Bob Aspell. Charlie volunteered his time at JACOA to work with those in treatment and transported clients to and from various treatment centers in Memphis, Tennessee sometimes going as far as Tupelo, Mississippi. During these transports, Charlie became incredibly impressed with the effectiveness of what was then called "halfway houses."

On May 13, 1979, *The Jackson Sun* published an Opinion Page letter Charlie wrote urging the community to support his passion for a halfway house. Charlie and Ruby Gay purchased three lots in the Fourth Ward of Jackson

Source: Madison County, Tennessee Assessors Office - 1972 Tax Map

(McCowat Street/North Highland Area) in July of 1979 for $39,500. Ironically, the law firm that prepared the deed for the lots was "Schneider, Schneider & Harris"; this is ironic because the daughter of the Schneiders and niece of Harris is Victoria Schneider Lake. Decades after this purchase, Lake will be instrumental in securing a substantial amount of funding that will expand T.A.M.B. to a nearly five-acre campus.

This purchase was the genesis of Charlie's laborious efforts to establish our T.A.M.B. of Jackson, our Aspell Manor. Charlie felt that if he could help men broken by alcoholism regain their dignity, self-worth, and productivity –it would be the most significant work of his life.

T.A.M.B. of Jackson was chartered on June 22, 1979, by Charlie Gay. It was the first step in establishing an additional local center for alcoholics that would provide detoxification, education, counseling, and group therapy. Gay transferred the three lots to T.A.M.B. in April/1981.

In an interview with *The Jackson Sun*, Charlie stated, *"The building will be used as a hall for about 20 recovering alcoholic men and is to be named Aspell Manor in honor of Bob Aspell."* At the time, Charlie estimated it would cost around $60,000 a year with an estimated cost of $300 a month per client. Aspell Manor would serve the 21 counties adjacent to Madison.

Source: *The Jackson Sun*, Tuesday, August 7, 1979.

In these early days of T.A.M.B., Charlie not only fought for funding but also community support. Alcoholics and addicts were deemed the 'unfortunates' in society Bob Aspell devoted his life to. Both Gay and Aspell knew what it was like to be marginalized and crippled by the disease of addiction. However, both were extremely grateful for those who reached out to the suffering alcoholic and addict with compassion. Both used what was freely given them to be a beacon of hope for others.

Sol Tuchfeld was an honorary board member and husband to the late Nancy Tuchfeld. He expressed the tremendous need for the center, and receiving services begins with asking for help and a willingness to participate. Aspell Manor was set to open September 1, 1979, at 331 North Highland Avenue. However, before the end of September, Charlie faced the zoning commission and the Highland Area Neighborhood Association (HANA). HANA expressed a sympathetic need for the center, just not in their neighborhood. HANA believed the center and the

Source: *The Jackson Sun*, September 21, 1979

Source: *The Jackson Sun*, October 31, 1979

unfortunates it would serve would be undesirable for the area. A strong endorsement and the much-needed boost to win approval by the Zoning board came from City Planning Director Gene Smith. Smith conducted extensive research on these types of halfway houses and their services, going as far as touring four different Memphis facilities. *"I came away with the belief that the homes were not objectionable, nor do they adversely affect neighboring property owners."* Smith went on to say that halfway houses are quite impressive, and the clients were there for a purpose.

Aspell Manor officially opened in November of 1979. Charlie Gay struggled for funding – for client services and the much-needed repairs to the old stately home. Charlie placed ads in the paper urging the community for support. He went before the city council and the county commission for funding, the United Way, and even auctioned off antiques and furnishings left behind in the old house. In 1980, Charlie was informed by P.F. Whitmore, then assistant commissioner of the Tennessee Division of Alcohol and Drug Abuse Services, that no funding would be available to new programs and a drastic cut to existing community Alcohol and Drug (A&D) programs was on the horizon. Whitmore attributed the cuts to federal plans to eliminate A&D block grant funding by 1982 and substantially decrease state appropriations for A&D programs. Furthermore, since Aspell had not secured matching local funds, this would nearly eliminate the small amount of federal and state revenue the organization was receiving.

According to Charlie, this left Aspell Manor with no other funding sources but confidently vowed, *"Aspell Manor will not close its doors. We are going to get the money."* Charlie proposed fifteen cent contributions from residents of the 21 counties that would benefit from the services offered at Aspell Manor. In November 1980, an anonymous donor committed a 'dollar for dollar' match, up to $10,000, for funds raised by December 31, 1980. During this time, the

Messiah Lutheran Church supported Aspell financially and encouraged others to do the same:

> *"It is our wish that others of our community – churches and individuals – could likewise be supportive. With continued funding more people could be reached, and better programming could begin. Aspell's program works! Men who once were enslaved are now being freed to live productive lives."*

Despite funding and zoning issues, Aspell Manor continued to report a reasonable success rate in restoring the alcoholic to a better life. Charlie noted that fifty-two men participated in the thirty-day program between November 1979 and June 1980 and forty-seven completed the program. Funding was slow – pennies at a time it seemed – but for the leadership within T.A.M.B., the most important thing was to provide a program of hope, love, and support.

T.A.M.B. leadership understood that getting a man sober and keeping him sober are two different things. Supporting this idea was when two of the non-complete clients returned on their own because they could not resist taking another drink, proving a seed was planted. Charlie said, *"If we don't accomplish completion the first time, we'll get him the second time. We do not ask them to come up to where we are. We go down to where they are, repeatedly so, if necessary."* Aspell Manor's program could get them sober and perhaps keep them sober, but only if they were willing to work for their recovery.

"A court may send a man to this program, but we can't make him go through it. Here, we can show a man how to live a normal life, but we can't make him live it."
– Bill Jenkins, Aspell counselor

Aspell Manor had around eight clients and used an adjoining lot to grow most of their fruits and vegetables. Aspell Manor staff in 1980 included: volunteer program director Charlie Gay, a part-time volunteer counselor/chaplain, a counselor paid a half-month salary, a cook, and a nighttime tech who earned room and board and about $100 a month. Fast forward to 2021, T.A.M.B. has more than sixty dedicated employees who are just as compassionate to the suffering alcoholic and addict as Bob Aspell and Charlie Gay were.

From the beginning, Charlie repeatedly stated that he would figure out a way to provide treatment services to women. In 1981, Charlie and the board pursued property located at 376 North Highland, less than half a mile from where Charlie's House is today. However, protestors and parking issues ultimately led to a denial of establishing a rehabilitation center for alcoholic women by the Jackson Board of Zoning.

Paul Mundt, then T.A.M.B. president, stated that they would continue to fight for a women's facility. Tommy Wilkerson, a staff member of Aspell at the time, said.

"It's just not fair letting the men get help and the women having to go without. I am not going to let up because I know these houses have been good for me, and there are women out there who are hurting as much as any man. They've got to have something to hang on to."

In a 1983 article declaring Aspell Manor has a future, it *warned* that if Aspell was to survive to see it, it would need to *'pare down its dream a bit,'* meaning services to women would need to defer until Aspell was strong enough to stand. It would be decades before Aspell would start treating women, and unbeknownst to Charlie Gay, Ann Middleton's sobriety during this time would prove to be an essential catalyst for women's services later.

In May 1980, *The Jackson Sun* did a story on Ann Middleton titled, *"On the Road to Recovery."* Ann was eager to share her story with whoever would listen, she had the drive to reach all the lonely people trying to tackle life from within a bottle.

"I don't have to drink to change the way I feel because now I like the way I feel. I don't know what life has in store, but I have no fear."
--- Ann Middleton

In recovery, Ann Middleton saw her mission as an

advocate for substance abuse treatment services for women. T.A.M.B. has been blessed that her mission led her and her beloved husband, Gus, to our campus. Dr. Gus and Ann Middleton would be

Source: *The Jackson Sun*, May 15, 1980

instrumental in establishing a sober living house and other programs for women on Aspell's campus. Ann fulfilled Charlie's promise to bring treatment to women in Jackson.

Charlie would spend the rest of his life honoring Bob Aspell. Charlie was not alone in this, on June 9, 1981, former Mayor Bob Conger proclaimed this day as *Bob Aspell Day*. A luncheon at the Civic Center was given in his honor, followed by an auction which raised more than $2,000. A University of Tennessee (UT) mat ended up in a bidding "*war*" between Mayor Bob Conger, City planner Gene Smith, and County Executive Walter Baker Harris. Wade Spire, director of Harbor House in Tupelo, Mississippi, told the 250 attendees,

> *"I guess if Bob Aspell were here today, Bob would probably say, in a very humble way, 'Don't concentrate too much on me, just get the job done.'"*

If Charlie Gay, Sr. was the catalyst in getting Aspell Manor and T.A.M.B. off the ground; why wouldn't he take all the credit? Why didn't he name the facility Charlie's Recovery Center? Why was it only after his passing that a building was named after him? Charlie had a character-rich mentor, Bob Aspell, who believed that those who light the lamppost merely produce the light and move on, they do not look back to see if their name is on the pole.

Charlie Edward Gay, Sr. died April 26, 1983, having shared all he had with the suffering alcoholics: his

Source: *The Jackson Sun*, April 27, 1983

experience, his strength, and his hope without regard to gender, race, or social standing. Harold Montgomery, Executive Director of JACOA at the time, described Charlie as having a gruff exterior.

However, it did not take long to discover a tender, loving heart just underneath it all. Charlie, emerging from his hell with alcoholism, dedicated his life to those who suffered. An illuminating legacy that still shines bright today.

CHAPTER THREE

Charlie Gay Transitional Living Facility
(Charlie's House)

Charlie's House in 2007

Simultaneously, as plans were being developed for a new administrative office, Luann Powell the Executive Director in 1993, and the Board were working on a project to purchase and renovate the old two-story Victorian, located at 341 North Highland, to expand recovery services. Powell proposed calling the home Charlie Gay Transitional Living Facility, "Charlie's House" for short, honoring Charlie Gay's legacy.

While this acquisition began in 1993, it would take nearly eight years and three Executive Directors for it to come to fruition. Lack of funding created numerous standstills for the program. Both a Supportive Housing Grant and HOME funds were applied for through the U.S. Department of Housing and Urban Development Grant (HUD), yet both denied. Subsequently, the head of Tennessee Housing Development Agency (THDA), John Johnson, encouraged Powell to submit a grant application because Johnson knew of funds available for such a program. However, as a backup plan, Powell worked closely with the local Community Development Block Grant (CDBG) office for funding opportunities.

Powell and the Board's efforts paid off. A grant through THDA for $67,000, and with funding from the CDBG, T.A.M.B. had $116,000 toward making Charlie's House a reality. The property at 341 North Highland was owned by W.J. Stewart who was approached with a purchase offer. Having worked on the administration building, Randy Nelson agreed to tour the old Victorian with an engineer to determine its suitability and determine if it was worth the $18,000 price tag. Nelson was so sure of the home's potential that he purchased the home for T.A.M.B. the day of the walkthrough, as well as recommended it for $114,000 in funding from the City Council. Nelson had a solid reputation, *"If you have Randy Nelson's support, more than likely you will receive the funding."* The timing of this expansion was perfect because the city was taking steps to clean up that area of North Highland Avenue.

With Nelson's recommendation, Powell asked the city for $114,000 to purchase and renovate the old Victorian, explaining that Aspell provided treatment services out of the property next door (Aspell Manor) with four dedicated beds to transitional living; a small attempt to keep clients in a recovery environment. Thus, the 341 North Highland property would create more space for housing clients who graduated from residential treatment and opening four more beds for those seeking treatment.

After a successful appraisal, a contract for $18,000 was drafted to purchase the home. However, the biggest challenge was awaiting the City Council's decision to provide funding for the property. T.A.M.B. closed on the property, without official word from the City, on November 12, 1993, and was slated for licensure on April 1, 1994. However, Charlie's House would rely on future Executive Director efforts to move the project along. Effective June 1, 1994, LuAnne Powell resigned as Executive Director to pursue other interests. Executive Directors J.C. Moore and Steve Patterson continued pursuing the Charlie's House program following Powell.

Finally, in 1998 Charlie's House experienced a surge. The Salvation Army, ironically an organization that Bob Aspell dedicated his life to, purchased the Senior Citizen's Center from the Jackson Housing Authority (JHA). Winston Henning and Linda Hopper with JHA verbally committed the proceeds from the sale to T.A.M.B. for Charlie's House final renovations. The City Council voted to spend the requested $114,000 on renovations for Charlie's House and began construction in the Fall of 1998. The agreement was that when the project was completed, they would turn the keys over to T.A.M.B. for one dollar and a 40-year lease.

Charlie's House in 2018

Charlie's house was completed around July of 1999 and started accepting residents in August. The program served a maximum of thirteen men agreeing to pay $75 per week, including one meal a day. All residents were subject to a drug screen upon admission and presented with rules and regulations for residing at Charlie's House. The program's goal was for clients to have a safe, affordable, and recovery supportive environment until they could transition back to the community, as Charlie Gay envisioned the program to provide.

On April 2, 2001, eighteen years after the passing of Charles Edward Gay, Sr., a ribbon-cutting ceremony was held on the steps of Charlie's House. Today, individuals in early recovery reside in the old Victorian home for the duration of Aspell's Intensive Outpatient Program (IOP), about eight to twelve weeks. Afterward, the client may move to other housing options on the campus, contingent on availability.

CHAPTER FOUR

1990 – 2004

John Shankle was Director of Aspell from 1983 until his retirement in 1990. In his final Director's Report on May 23, 1990, he reflected on his time with Aspell. At the time he was considering the Director position, he asked a friend who had been involved in A&D service delivery for over twenty years,

> *"What should I do about going to work at Aspell Manor?"*
> *She replied, "It is an experience you must not miss."*

During Shankle's administration, he increased the United Way funding from $10,000 to $17,000 in 1983. Shankle praised the United Way for funding; without it and a $20,000 donation from an anonymous donor, Aspell could

not have stayed in operation. Shankle and another staff member sacrificed a month's salary to ensure the program could continue without interruption.

A major complaint with the community and funders was the perception that Aspell and JACOA was an unnecessary duplication of services, and thus funding both were financially redundant. However, both Shankle and Harold Montgomery (JACOA) touted this as an unfortunate and indirect funding competition. Shankle explained both programs need funding because *"There are more drunks than there are beds to serve them."* Today, capacity is still an ongoing issue.

In 1990, Shankle and the Board attempted to purchase property at 201 Ash Street (previously Hillcrest Baptist Church) for additional space or even to replace the old Victorian structure at 331 North Highland. In his letter to the former assistant commissioner, George Riggall, he stated, *"the structure – despite its charm – continues to require constant time and money to house our existing program."* Furthermore, Shankle said the local Historical Zoning Commission posed a challenge to alleviate the current space constraints and making even minor modifications to the Victorian structure a nearly impossible barrier. Ultimately, the board decided 201 Ash Street was more work than benefit.

Even after retiring, Shankle would continue to serve on the Board of Directors, and in January 1995, was elected President of the Board. Tommy Grady took over as Executive Director in September of 1990. During the 1989-1990 fiscal year, T.A.M.B. had twelve employees. Among them was an Executive Director and an Associate Director; however, with extreme budget cuts and talks of eliminating third shift monitoring, the board decided that the two positions would not be supported by the budget and merged them into one. During Grady's administration, several properties were pursued to increase capacity – The Care Center, Tinker Hill, 351 North Liberty, and Rosenblum Drive property. With each pursuit, the Board met to ensure the use of any property would not jeopardize Aspell's original mission.

In 1991, Grady approached Gary Deaton, President of the Board for The Care Center, with a need to lease the property. Grady's primary concern and use for the property was to ensure that clients were not lost during the wait for a bed at Aspell Manor. Grady wrote,

"Much too often, a client will seek admission at the Manor, but no bed is available. By the time a bed becomes available, the client cannot be found, and there have been instances where clients have died waiting for a bed."

Leasing the Care Center would provide a 'pre-admission/post-admission' facility for clients to enter while on Aspell's waitlist. Aspell's enduring philosophy is to keep clients within a recovery environment for as long as possible to safeguard the longevity of their sobriety.

A significant budget issue came when alcohol and drug programs were transitioned from the Tennessee Department of Mental Health and Mental Retardation (TDMHMR) to the Tennessee Department of Public Health (TDPH). TDMHMR provided funds upfront with signed contracts. In contrast, TDPH provided payments after services rendered and billing processed through the state. Additionally, during this time, political ideologies were turning away from A&D issues to environmental ones. Grady was told that this shift in legislative priorities would become a viable threat for A&D funding to run out by 1994.

Tommy Grady had worked for Aspell since 1989 and was the Executive Director from September 1990 to September 1991. When Grady submitted his resignation, the Board had a challenging time filling the position. They hired Victor Vescovo in September of 1991, and he resigned a month later. Shankle was appointed to return as Executive Director until a new director was hired. In November 1991, the board interviewed: Luanne Powell, Malcolm Mosier, and David Matlock. On December 6, 1991, the Board offered the position to Powell, and she began serving Aspell as the Executive Director on January 2, 1992.

Aspell around 1979

Aspell around 1995

Aspell 2020

Powell's dream was BIG: *"What I would like to do is for us to look at a long-range plan of the needs of the Manor. We are not going to be simply Aspell Manor any longer. It is going to be larger than that. I propose that since we will encompass three buildings to have a name change that reflects who we are. I suggest that we change the name to Aspell Recovery Center, leaving the big house as Aspell Manor."*

Powell's administration faced the continued challenge of capacity and the evolving decline of the Aspell Manor building, specifically the $18,000 price tag for a much-needed roof repair, leaks, interior damage, and nearly $5,000 foundation damage. At one point, Powell suggested, *"there's more tape than carpet,"* regarding flooring in Aspell Manor.

"People are coming in right off the streets, asking for help and literally have nothing to offer or possess. We are known for not turning anyone away, but this is becoming quite a difficult task. We are so crowded that we are pushing out the walls."

The condition of Aspell Manor continued to plague state audits. Board discussions included building a new building or approaching Dr. Hyran Barefoot with Union University and Dr. Alex Leech, county executive, for the use of the old Union Campus located between College Street and Lexington Avenue. Ultimately, the Board agreed with Powell, they needed to develop an expansion strategy.

Powell was approached in March of 1993 with a unique and possibly controversial plan. Steven Xanthopoulos, attorney, and Executive Director of West Tennessee Legal Services, called Powell to see if she would be interested in hosting an AIDS bed in West Tennessee. Aspell was the first place Xanthopoulos pitched the request that Aspell reserve one bed for an AIDS patient dealing with addiction, suggesting up to $20,000 could be contributed if Powell, and the Board, agreed. Powell and Charlie Heiser, Program Director at the time, decided it would be great for Aspell and the community if they could make this commitment. They proposed using the 14th bed (emergency bed) in the Manor and were adamant the person would remain anonymous as any other protected client.

E. Wallace Jones Administration Building

In May 1992, Powell targeted the lot behind the old Manor for administrative offices. Powell suggested, "*With the new Administration Building, I propose that we call it the Wallace Jones Administration Building in honor of former board member Wallace Jones. I have already talked with some interested people that would donate money in his honor. I think that with a name attached to it with someone as honorable as Mr. Jones, we would stand a remarkable chance of being able to go into this building debt-free.*"

Powell and the Board approached Xanthopoulos and Randy Nelson with the Community Development Office because some block grant funding or low-interest loans would help build an administrative office. These funds were used to create and renovate office space for the Center for Adult Reading and Enrichment and renovation of office space for the United Way, both here in Jackson, Tennessee.

Plans were drawn, redrawn, and finally submitted to Brown and Dedmon Construction Company for a new administration building on March 22, 1993. Initially, the plan was to place a laundry area in the building, but that would pose a substantial challenge to the much-needed storage space. Powell decided storage was more important and the laundry area could replace the old Manor's kitchen set-up; a kitchenette was already part of the new administration building.

On June 1, 1993, T.A.M.B. secured a $50,000 construction loan from First Tennessee Bank to purchase and construct a new administration building on the lot located at 115 McCowat Street. On March 25, 1994, Aspell Recovery Center hosted a crowded and complimentary open house for the E. Wallis Jones Administration Building.

E. Wallis Jones Administration Building

In 1993, Powell and the Board pursued TennCare contracts. Due to the potential and substantial cuts to A&D program federal funding, they felt it necessary to look at other funding streams. During this time, A&D funds were being carved out of the TennCare program. Like today, managed care organizations expected highly credentialed staff (M.D., Ph.D.) to sign off on medical records, something the Aspell budget could not support.

Luanne Powell served as Executive Director from January 2, 1992, to June 1, 1994. During her administration, Powell and the Board completed some much-needed renovations to Aspell Manor, built an administration building, and secured a substantial amount of funding to create Charlie's House. Additionally, Powell began the 'Employee Appreciation' push by approaching the Board to recognize the hard work and dedication of Charlie Heiser and Gerald Cupples, both having served Aspell for ten consecutive years. Charlie Heiser died May 23, 2006, still serving the mission of Aspell. Heiser oversaw Charlie's House and provided support for those early in recovery. Powell continued to serve on the Board, becoming Treasurer in January 1995. In 2019, Powell returned to the Aspell Board of Directors.

J.C. Moore accepted the Executive Director position on June 20, 1994. His first order of business was Charlie's House. Despite numerous advertisements for bids to complete the renovations, bids were slow to come. Meanwhile, Moore continued to implement the program that would ultimately become Charlie's House by visiting similar facilities. For example, Moore met with Jim Ward, who ran a halfway house in Oxford, Mississippi. Ward ran a strict, yet successful program that Moore utilized in drafting the "Rules and Regulations" for Charlie's House. Ward suggested that a critical component in his plan was hiring a Transitional House Manager, someone who lived in the home to maintain control and order. Additionally, "rules and regulations" must be presented to, and signed off by, the client as it created a written statement of accountability and acknowledgment of rights and responsibilities. Rent statements were officially drafted and presented to clients weekly.

Clients in early recovery, particularly right out of residential treatment (a controlled environment whereby all physiological needs are met – food, shelter, water), faced a daunting situation as they transition back into society. With the tools they learned in residential, coupled with the limited freedoms of a program like Charlie's House, it only enhanced their recovery success. Clients who continue to develop recovery life skills such as budgeting and employment stand a better chance of sustaining long-term sobriety. Paying rent was just part of that transition back to society as a productive and accountable member.

In 1994, Moore approached the Board to install a fence to provide better security for the small but growing campus. Of course, the fence would be another trip before the historical commission. Moore also expressed a need for a van to transport clients from Aspell Manor to outside events, including local recovery meetings. A used van with 120,000 miles on it, was approved for purchase by the board. A few obstacles emerged with this endeavor: liability insurance cost would go from $300,000 to close to a million dollars in coverage, van maintenance expense, and approaching Union University to store the van until all challenges have been overcome. Moore had already been in discussions with Union University, Gary Carter, to allow individuals going into transitional living an opportunity to work for the college. Clients have been working for Jim Miles occasionally and have been working out fine.

During Moore's administration, he pursued controllable funding streams, such as an attempt to start a DUI School on the Aspell property. Moore proposed conducting evaluations for the Board of Corrections and hosting workshops at Aspell for a fee-per-attendee. Obtaining a National Association of Alcoholism and Drug Abuse Counselors (NAADAC) membership could remedy the liability insurance dilemma because, according to Moore, NAADAC could potentially furnish the liability policy for a fraction of the $1,619 annual fee quoted by Steve Little with Cornerstone Insurance Company.

Moore instituted a clinical treatment team to review weekly goals and progress of clients and a Clinical Review Committee. The Review Committee was responsible for charting documentation and other state-mandated clinical directives. During this time, there was a need for a more intensive outpatient program than Aftercare and Family groups; however, required highly qualified staff to provide.

Effective March 31, 1995, J.C. Moore resigned as Executive Director and his employment with T.A.M.B. After numerous interviews, Steve Patterson accepted the position of Executive Director and Charlie Heiser as Clinical Director. There was a great need for an updated "Policies and Procedures" manual and an organization-wide need for computer literacy education.

Steve Patterson was officially named Executive Director in May 1995. The constant need to serve more clients with less capacity became a point of contention with the state during the mid-1990s. With the Department of Health, Debbie Roberson informed Patterson that the program should define a length of stay, rather than 'open-ended,' suggesting a definition of 30-days. Roberson, representing the state, wanted T.A.M.B. to serve around 144 clients a year. To do this, Patterson suggested tightening up the length of stay in the Manor and aggressively pursue an outpatient program, primarily since the administration building was already licensed for such a program. The T.A.M.B. administration collaborated with the local vocational rehabilitation center for a joint effort with Aspell Recovery Center to provide outpatient services.

There was a push to get members of the local criminal justice systems on campus (judges, probation officers, and others) to educate them and experience Aspell's programs firsthand. The outpatient program had received little interest as most of the clients were court-ordered to licensed programs. A contract with Cumberland Heights to use space at Aspell to deliver services was signed with a six-month trial run. The collaboration boosted publicity, an additional partnership with a successful and established A&D program, a valuable learning experience, and an introduction to the managed care concept. The outpatient program started on December 1, 1997.

In May 1995, Patterson welcomed new employees, including Truman Masters. Masters came to Aspell from Tru Recovery in Bolivar where he worked in treatment for four years. Patterson stated to the Board, *"We are very proud he (Masters) has associated himself with our agency."* A sentiment that would be expressed for decades to come.

Patterson pressed to have more representation in the courts, noting that when the Courts sent someone to treatment, they usually sent money to cover it. During this time, Charlie Heiser made trips to meet with United Way counties, traveled to meet with state officials and Tennessee Alcohol and Drug Association (TADA) meetings in Nashville to advocate for and represent Aspell. Patterson advocated for an improvement in outreach services for IV users, incorporated infection control and universal precaution measures, enacted a drug-free workplace agreement, and reviewed and updated the entire policies and procedures manual. During this time, a Christmas Bonus' was issued for the first time: $100 for full-time and $50 for part-time staff.

A significant part of the long-range plan was to strategize a balance of treatment beds and transitional beds to meet demand. At the time, discussions revolved around obtaining a "floating" halfway house license and continued attempts to secure a TennCare contract. The challenge was that if by July 1998 no state contracts were in place, then no block grant funding would be secured. The other option was to increase private pay for a flat $2,400 for 28 days of treatment or merge with another treatment center (i.e., JACOA or Jack Gene). The board would not consider such a merger. At the time, there were only 71 beds between the three centers (Aspell, JACOA., and Jack Gene) to serve the 21 counties outside Shelby. The ultimate strategy was for Aspell to achieve sustainable funding balanced with client census.

Patterson identified the need for more qualified counselors and education funding for the current ones. Truman Masters, treatment director, completed his A&D Counselor certification through the University of Georgia. Masters was responsible for verifying the completeness and accuracy of documentation in other counselors' charts and providing ongoing education opportunities. Counselor, Rick Lutrell was enrolled in an Alcohol and Drug Certification course at Shelby State in Memphis. Patterson's education program for staff was that Aspell would pay $100 a semester for a B average. Additionally, David Johnson conducted training at Aspell on the "12 Core Functions."

Aspell was getting a technological make-over with new computers and new phone systems. Computers, printers, and program training, such as Office 97, was estimated to cost around $10,000 with the new phone system around $2,600. An air purifier was installed in the administration building to allow for smoking indoors; neither clients nor staff would need to be outdoors after dark. Some of these upgrades were paid for by a one-time grant of $14,550 by the state. A "Client Intake" system was established through the public health departments. Block grant funding continued to be paid upfront, versus 'fee for service' after the fact.

Aspell was listed with the State Resource Directory and was getting referrals. However, at the end of the 97-98 fiscal year, the census was around four; some administrative staff said this was typical for year-end. The aftercare program was going well during this time, with a census of ten to eleven attending the once-a-week session. The program allowed former clients to demonstrate a willingness to process recovery and personal concerns that were often hindered in open community meetings.

A house donated to Aspell several years earlier, 173 E. Deadrick Street, was offered back to the donor, Bernard M. Malloy. While being rented, the property did not bring in enough revenue to offset the cost of owning it. After much back and forth, the Mallory family was convinced to donate the property to Barry Walker, who was involved in a significant renovation project nearby.

A 1999 Van, clear of any logos or otherwise identifiable agency markings was purchased to transport clients; the old van was sold for $2,000. A break-in of the administration building prompted Patterson and the board to install security bars on the windows and security lighting. Aspell was awarded one of the "Best Treatment Centers" by the State Bureau at the end of 1999.

In the new millennium, new goals included increased marketing via materials such as brochures, radio ads, and visits to other healthcare providers. Recreational activities for clients were a priority. A proposal was drafted to acquire an adjacent lot for a recreational facility. Clients would enjoy recreational activities to build their stability in social activities without using drugs and alcohol. Employee education and training remained an ongoing objective. The next goal for Charlie's House was licensure, which would bring in additional revenue per resident. Aspell Manor needed some serious upkeep and repairs. Staff salaries were increased, and the Christmas bonus rose to $200 for full-time and $100 for part-time. Ann Middleton returned to the Board of Directors. There were eleven staff members by the end of 2000.

Strategic plans for 2001-2002 included expansion of the downstairs office space by renovating the attic, creating a receptionist area downstairs. Avenues to provide indigent outpatient services were researched, monthly clinical in-service training, supportive efforts to help counselors achieve licensure, and administrative staff support toward more education. The board approved a 4% cost of living raise in January 2001.

An Intensive Outpatient Program (IOP) was initiated and developed as a pilot program, on a one-year trial basis. IOP, in addition to regularly scheduled meetings with counselors, would run four evenings a week, three-hour sessions each. The program would serve Charlie's House residents and clients from the community. In May 2001, J.C. Moore returned to Aspell to head up the IOP Program.

In 2002, T.A.M.B. purchased property located at 119 McCowat Street. The home required a complete renovation. However, it was a good purchase and one step closer to securing the campus we have today. The property is located next door to the administration building.

By the end of 2004, T.A.M.B., while financially stable, the organization faced severe problems with its annual state Board of Health compliance audit. Furthermore, the area around the treatment programs was polluted with criminal activity, including prostitution and drug transactions. It became glaringly apparent that changes were needed.

Long time Board members Ann Middleton and Regina Saffel had always advocated putting our client's needs first, a reminder that would soon become a concrete mission statement. A promise to treat the underprivileged and the indigent; to always be a beacon of hope for those who fight the disease of addiction.

CHAPTER FIVE

2005-2020

"God never said our blessings wouldn't be burdens sometimes. It's all about how you choose to handle the challenge."
– Tammy Yosich

A new era began for Aspell in 2005; the Board hired a new Executive Director, Richard Barber, who found himself overseer of an organization whose beacon was all but extinguished. Barber would be responsible for facilitating a vision of growth and expansion for the darkening organization. At the start of Barber's administration, Aspell had a budget of around $450,000, a staff of eleven, and starting his second day at the helm, an unannounced return of the state licensure team. The state licensure returned to check on the progress of a less than glowing audit six months earlier. Anyone else might have turned and ran, but Barber did not because he knew the Board's passion and the compassion of the small but dedicated staff. Nearly nineteen years sober and a long history of working in treatment, quitting was not an option for Barber.

Barber defined T.A.M.B. by drafting a Mission, Vision, and Value statement that educated the community on exactly what the organization stood for, how it would pursue opportunities for growth, the clients, and supporters, and a clear vision for the road ahead.

MISSION STATEMENT
Aspell will reach out to the suffering alcoholic, addict, and those with a co-occurring disorder with compassion, always mindful of the trust of the community.

VISION STATEMENT:
The vision of Aspell is to create accessible addiction treatment services, which are client/family focused, outcome driven, and cost efficient.

VALUE STATEMENT:
Respect for our clients, for referring agencies and for each other.
Integrity, not to be compromised regardless of reason
Open-minded: will not be judgmental and will not practice contempt prior to investigation
Spirituality: our conduct will be evidence of our belief in a power greater than ourselves.

Barber initiated an annual staff outing early in his administration, where staff and spouses gathered off-campus for food and fellowship. This yearly event started in late 2005. In June of 2007, the event was titled *"Soberstock"* and has been held on Aspell's campus ever since. It is organized and put on by Aspell alumni, headed up by Frankie Elliott.

Barber's dedication to staff development and inclusion was essential, and the implementation of a quality council was in the making within two weeks of Barber taking over as Executive Director. In January of 2007, the Quality Council's first meeting was held to discuss all aspects of the organization, including clinical, administrative, and Board Meeting discussions. For Barber, the staff was the organization's strength, those who conduct the day-to-day operations within their respective departments. In this vein,

Barber – like Powell earlier – felt that staff should be honored for their passion and dedication to the organization as they reached service milestones. In January of 2006, Aspell hosted its first *Annual Employee Appreciation Banquet.* The evening included a dinner and a speaker chosen by the Quality Council.

T.A.M.B. was funded only by a Block Grant (around $325,000 a year) and ADAT[2] ($5,000 a year) that came from the state that paid $110 a day per client, and at the time, the census was around eight to nine men in Aspell Manor. Charlie's House was funded by rent paid by residents and Block Grant reimbursement of $55 per day for IOP clients. A significant financial boost came in 2005 with a $25,000 contribution from the Meredith Estate, $50,000 from West Tennessee Healthcare and a $19,000 bump in Block Grant revenue.

T.A.M.B. initiated a strategic plan to expand capacity and further enhance the services offered. Aspell Recovery Center consisted of four lots: Aspell Manor, the Administration Building, McCowat House, and Charlie's House. Yet, amazingly despite the obstacles, Barber and the Board saw a glowing vision of a fruitful campus.

---

[2] Alcohol and Drug Addiction Treatment Fund

In 2005, funding was secured to renovate the property at 119 McCowat Street. By July, McCowat House, as it was called, had three residents. The home provided a step-down

McCowat House in 2018

living arrangement for those completing Charlie's House; while McCowat House had some rules and regulations, it was less intense than those in transitional housing. This home paved the way for residents to continue to live in a structured recovery environment while continuing to make progress toward transitioning to independent living in the community.

Unfortunately, Mrs. Regina Saffel had to resign from the Board of Directors after twelve years of dedicated service (1993-2005) due to health issues. Mrs. Saffel was a loyal and dedicated member of Aspell's Board of Directors. During her tenure, Aspell experienced a tremendous period of growth and renewal. Mrs. Saffel's tireless and selfless commitment to others is a shining example of *The Golden Rule*, a rule she lived by and promoted. In 2005, she received the *Tennessee Volunteer of the Year Award* at the State Capitol Building in Nashville because of her relentless volunteer spirit. Additionally, Diana McConnell, with Court

Appointed Special Advocate (CASA) stated, *"Mrs. Saffel is our best volunteer and mostly handle medically fragile children."* Saffel lived her faith, and because of her service to Aspell and her community, the world is a better place.

In the summer of 2005, T.A.M.B. purchased 132 Talbot Street for $35,000. Since 1979, there has been a drive to provide services to women. Finally, in August of 2007, a significant grant was announced and a new commitment that included providing services to women

Life House in 2018

struggling with addiction was made. At first, it was a tad uncomfortable stepping outside our traditional male constituency. As research has shown, and our women clients have revealed, there is more complexity among women and addiction than has been demonstrated in men.

Aspell Recovery Center now offering services to women

Source: *The Jackson Sun*, August 19, 2017

In the first month, Life House had a full census with a significant waiting list. This left no doubt about the need for such a program, as the new women's residential facility remained full. Within a relatively short time, T.A.M.B. was able to secure a valuable and vital resource that is reflected in our mission statement, "...the trust of the community." This was possible because of the bipartisan support from diverse state and local leaders who were able to help secure a $250,000 grant from the state to continue women's services.

Despite all the challenges of 2005, Barber and his team went into action and corrected all default areas of the previous audit. Evidence of the team's hard work was the state licensing board letter stating, "We are pleased to advise you that no deficiencies were cited as a result of the state health licensure survey conducted at your facility on July 31, 2006". Aspell was beginning to show signs of renewed life and growth. Her dimmed light was starting to burn a little brighter.

Starting in January of 2005, Barber and the Board

Talbot House in 2015

worked on acquiring and updating property located at 130 Talbot Street, soon to be called Talbot House. Federal Home Loan Bank of Cincinnati (FHLB) funding was applied for but initially denied. Still, leadership refused to give up and reapplied early 2006.

In August of 2006, Aspell received funding through the FHLB to acquire and renovate Talbot House. The Bank of Jackson provided a bridge (construction) loan to start work on the property. Talbot House was built in the mid-1930s to 1940s and became a long-term sober-living facility for up to six men in early recovery. This was one of the first expansion successes that Dr. Victoria (Vicki) Lake would bring to T.A.M.B. of Jackson, TN.

On October 9, 2007, a ribbon-cutting ceremony was held for Talbot House, and the outstanding effort between T.A.M.B., the Bank of Jackson, and the FHLB that made this expansion possible for those facing homelessness and chemical dependency. FHLB is a banking institution not associated with the Federal Government but is required by legislation to use a portion of its profits for community housing grants.

Talbot House (2007) Ribbon Cutting with Mrs. Ann Middleton (sitting in green blouse).

A Jackson/Madison County crime task force was established in 2007 to look for ways to alleviate the overcrowded city and county jails. The primary goal was to look at non-violent inmates that could benefit from rehabilitation efforts and be released. Dr. Lake chaired the task force committee and invited area organizations to become members. The group's main topic revolved around repeat offenders, especially those with an unaddressed drug or alcohol issue that became caught in the revolving door of

Group discusses reforming criminals

Source: *The Jackson Sun*, September 11, 2007

the criminal justice system. These individuals, many of whom faced recidivism because businesses were unfriendly to ex-convicts, needed help. Barber welcomed the invitation to serve as a member and agreed that there should be more rehabilitation programs at the jails. Unemployment often leads to poverty, and without means to care for themselves or their families, many of the released inmates would return to criminal activity. In a room full of business owners and leaders, only two reported they hired ex-convicts. Former Jackson Police Chief Rick Staples responded, *"So we've got two in a room full of employers. We have a problem."*

In 2009, additional funding came from securing a TennCare contract with three Managed Care organizations. TennCare enrollees now had access to the continuum of care services offered at Aspell. At the time, only 20 percent of those seeking treatment could access it, so with the ability to accept TennCare clients, Aspell was able to open its doors to more individuals seeking treatment.

Expansion efforts increased because as more clients were being admitted and moving through the programs and housing options, it was imperative to create more independent living opportunities. Dr. Lake wrote and secured additional grant funding from the FHLB to purchase the apartment complex located at 218 Talbot Street, aptly named Talbot Towers.

> *"Affordable living is one of the most difficult things in early recovery. This is a big step in offering stability."*
> – Richard Barber, July 29, 2009 Interview with *The Jackson Sun*

The FHLB grant of $501,000 for the purchase and renovation of Talbot Towers could mean the difference between a full, successful life and no life at all. The clients that completed the continuum of care, fighting hard for their recovery, deserved to remain in an environment conducive to

sustainable sobriety and support systems. Talbot Towers meant families could be reunited, and single individuals had a safe place to go after treatment rather than back to respective communities, which often proved to be unhealthy and unsupportive.

This was precisely the type of atmosphere recovering addicts needed to stabilize their lives after treatment. Furthermore, with the apartments within view of Aspell's campus, those entering residential treatment have a front row seat to what sobriety will look like over the course of a year; at three months as individuals move from Charlie's House to McCowat or Talbot House, at six months to a year as those individuals move to Talbot Towers. Even years of

Our View PAGE 11A • THE JACKSON SUN • FRIDAY, JULY 31, 2009

Aspell expansion is good for community

It is good news for Jackson and other West Tennessee communities that the Aspell Recovery Center is expanding. Providing community-based treatment for drug and alcohol addiction has always been an uphill battle in Jackson. But it is a critically important community service for those who need help battling these addictions. A center such as Aspell can mean the difference between a full, successful life and no life at all.

Aspell received a $301,000 federal grant that will enable the center to purchase the 36-unit Talbot Towers apartment complex adjacent to its present facilities. The apartments will be renovated to become a drug- and alcohol-free place for recovering addicts to live after completing Aspell's recovery program. Units will be available to anyone who meets the income requirement.

Aspell staff will manage the apartment complex and help ensure that it stays drug and alcohol free. In fact, people renting the units will have to sign an agreement saying they will not use alcohol or drugs. This is the kind of living atmosphere recovering addicts need in order to help stabilize their lives after treatment.

There was a time when drug and alcohol addiction treatment was not available in Jackson. Addicts were shunned, even by the medical community. Fortunately, medical professionals began to understand these addictions were a sickness, not simply a moral failure of its victims. Treatment programs slowly emerged and facilities such as Aspell were created by caring local residents. Today, the Aspell Recovery Center helps carry on this important community-based treatment for those afflicted by addition.

Aspell's recovery program goes beyond the usual 28-day treatment protocols offered by many facilities. Such programs are limited to reflect what medical insurance programs are willing to pay for. Aspell offers a long-term residential treatment protocol. The new apartment facility will be a natural extension of this approach offering recovering addicts an affordable, safe environment in which to live as they extend their recovery.

Source: *The Jackson Sun*, July 31, 2009

sustained sobriety, as we have seen individuals and families move from Talbot Towers to homes of their own. Talbot Towers was a significant achievement in expansion and secured an area once overrun with blight and crime.

Today, Talbot Towers continues to be a refuge for recovery, tenants sign a lease like any other apartment complex; however, with this lease, they also agree to remain clean and sober, not allow drugs or alcohol to be brought onto the property by themselves or any of their guests. They decide to become a part of a tenant association dedicated to the complex's safe, supportive, and serene environment.

Over the past eleven years, many tenants moved into an apartment, often the first place of their own, either by themselves, a roommate, or significant other. We have witnessed them engage in Talbot Towers activities and with their fellow residents, making sure the property is safe and supportive. This is the apartment building's ultimate purpose for single individuals and families to sustain their

Talbot Towers in 2018

sobriety and independence, transitioning fully into society well-adjusted, productive, and genuine community members. For many, their journey started once they were admitted to Aspell's residential program.

In 2009, Aspell was honored with the *"Outstanding On-Site Feeding Program"* award by the Mid-South Food Bank. As one can imagine, feeding twelve men (2005) three meals a day plus snack options can be a challenge, but, since 2005, we have met that challenge with grace. Today, Alma

Delk and a part-time cook serve up nearly 126 delicious, hand-crafted meals every day. It is impressive that Alma can shop for, prepare, and serve meals to nearly 45 people, three times a day.

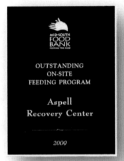

In 1981, former Mayor Bob Conger declared June 9 as *"Aspell Manor Day,"* honoring the late Bob Aspell, and on November 3, 2009, former Mayor Jerry Gist declared that day as *"Aspell Recovery Center Day."*

Every day is one more day to honor those who come to us for help and show them unconditional love until they can begin to love themselves. For both declared "Days," it is the compassion and dedication of people involved in the efforts to reach out to the suffering alcoholic, addict, and those with co-occurring disorders that earn the recognition. Today, as it was in 2009 and will be for years, we are continuing the legacy Bob Aspell started when he first arrived in Jackson, Tennessee in 1954. Like Bob, we always remain mindful of the community's trust.

Aspell's community awareness continued to increase, and in 2010 received the Pinnacle Award within the large nonprofit category, a category going into the new millennium certainly did not seem possible. At the Pinnacle Award ceremony, then Board member Charlie Allison said, *"In 2005, we thought we were going to have to close the place because challenges were threatening our funding with the state audits."* Bold changes that occurred in 2005 secured Aspell to remain not only relevant but provided a platform for growth.

On October 22, 2010, a radiant lamppost lighter, Mrs. Ann Middleton, passed from this world's light to the

Ann and her husband Gus Middleton

magnificent glow of Heaven. The light of hope, compassion, and love cannot be extinguished with the passing of our loved ones, for it remains a flickering flame that provides a constant glow for travelers. Ann's glow will continue to live on through the lives she touched while here, and through every woman who will reside in the home dedicated to her legacy.

Ann was feisty and confident; she was known for her compassion to help those who struggled with addiction. With her husband alongside her, Ann fought her own battle with alcoholism and decided it would be her life's mission to help as many struggling with the same affliction. Ann did this with grace and gratitude. Ann was an avid supporter of Aspell as a board member and a member of the recovery community since the founding of T.A.M.B. in 1979.

Ann Middleton's legacy with Aspell will live forever. Before her passing, Ann and her family made a significant gift to Aspell. Ann wanted to ensure that women in early recovery had a safe and supportive environment to  practice the principles of recovery. The property located at 131 McCowat Street was renovated and became a haven for women in early recovery, rightly named Ms. Ann's House. The home continues to house up to eight women in early recovery in a loving, safe, and supportive setting. A sign on the door reads: *"Ms. Ann's House – Love is understanding whether or not you approve."*

> *"This is the kind of place that gave Ann back her life and gave us back our lives. Our family is dedicated to the mission of helping people recover through the 12-step program."*
> ---Gus Middleton, 2011 *The Jackson Sun* interview

Since 1979, T.A.M.B. was strictly a substance abuse treatment center; other than a client requesting outside services to a mental health professional, services were limited to treating the disease of addiction. However, in

April of 2010, Aspell was visited by a state consultant with suggestions for becoming co-occurring capable by July 2011. The purpose of moving treatment centers into a co-occurring capable arena, rather than single service substance abuse, is that with addiction and mental health it is difficult to ascertain which one came first. In other words, is a person depressed because of their drug use, or were they depressed and used alcohol and/or drugs to self-medicate? By simultaneously treating both–the mental health and substance abuse issues–the client became better suited for recovery and less likely to relapse. By the first of the 2011-2012 fiscal year, Aspell was co-occurring capable and received a small bump in residential treatment per diem rate from $110 to $119.

By 2012, T.A.M.B. had renovated several properties, and the campus was starting to take shape. Cedar House

115 Cedar Street

located at 115 Cedar Street was acquired and renovated, creating additional space for recovering clients to live on campus. The property also had a garage apartment for additional independent living. A house bought a few years earlier located at 114 Talbot Street was demolished due to its deteriorated condition, and green space was created. With more campus residents, meant more people were getting involved with the annual *Soberstock* event.

During 2012, the first alumni association meeting was held, and with all the improvements on the campus, Aspell was being recognized and supported by the community.

Hal Crocker, Crocker Construction, handwrote a heartfelt letter of support to Aspell. In part, Crocker wrote, *"I was impressed by the work Aspell Manor is doing. I believe the work you are doing is important to our community. I am glad to have you as our neighbor for our Healthy Community/Jackson Walk Project."*

In 2017, we received an email from neighbors on Clay and Deadrick Streets who said they have watched our campus grow over the years. With the construction going on around the downtown area and our beautiful and stable campus on the other side, they said, *"we now have the best neighbors one could ever hope for. Thanks for being such a good neighbor."*

As mentioned earlier, Aspell Manor was not always a welcomed member of the neighborhood. However, with proven treatment results, just as much dedication to cleaning up the area as any other invested citizen, and the compassionate services we provide shows that our positive presence in the Lambuth Area Neighborhood Association (LANA) was unmistakably felt throughout the city of Jackson. Additionally, we earned the 2012 Mayor's Civic Pride Award for the renovations, giving more credence to the heartfelt dedication Aspell was spreading throughout the community. If we were feeling the love at the community level, we were also feeling it on the national level.

In 2013, Aspell was designated a Top 50 nonprofit place to work in the United States by the *NonProfit Times* and the *Best Companies Group.* This designation is exceptionally competitive, and we were up against incredible organizations like the Wounded Warrior Project and St. Jude Children's Research Hospital. The award was based on a 72 confidential questionnaire completed by the organization's staff, making the award even more special. It spoke volumes about Aspell staff, their belief in their work, and the organization they love.

WEDNESDAY, APRIL 3, 2013 • THE JACKSON SUN

SECTION B, PAGE 4

Local non profit gets national acclaim

The Jackson Sun

Aspell Recovery Center has been designated as a Top 50 non profit place to work in the United States by the NonProfit Times and the Best Companies Group, according to a news release. The NonProfit Times is a national publication reaching over 85,000 non profit executives.

Source: *The Jackson Sun, April 3, 2013*

"It sheds a light on Aspell," Barber stated in 2013 after accepting the David Hallock Memorial Award for his work as Aspell's Executive Director. Barber's statement is true whether we are, as an organization, earning an award for excellence or an individual staff member. The day-to-day work continues, and recognition is not the goal. However, when it happens, it illuminates the hard work and dedication of not just those directly involved with Aspell but a dynamic collaboration within the community and the state of Tennessee that has backed our efforts since 1979.

In 2014, the Tennessee Medical Association (TMA) recognized Aspell with the TMA Community Service Award. This prestigious award is presented to individuals and organizations that the TMA board feels is making significant contributions to our state's health and well-being and the community they serve. The recognition adds one more bulb to the beacon of hope burning at Aspell.

Increasing benefits to staff has always been part of Board Meetings since 1979, and in 2005, the topic of offering a retirement plan was discussed. In 2015, Barber and the Board of Directors worked out a way to offer a retirement plan option to full-time employees. T.A.M.B. also matches employee contributions up to 3%. This new retirement program went over well with all staff, young and old, and with healthcare costs already covered for staff, it made life easier.

Nonprofits attempt to be competitive in their employee's pay rate, but sometimes budgets and the ebb and flow of revenue impede yearly increases. To date, Aspell has maintained health insurance on full-time employees, continued the match of up to 3% on retirement contributions, provided a 3% cost of living increase or a merit raise each year, up to a 3% incentive bonus based on meeting yearly set goals, and continues to issue Christmas Bonuses. This ability to provide excellent benefits to staff could not possibly happen without the dynamic and proactive leadership that governs Aspell.

Renovating properties continued into 2015 with the acquisition and rehabilitation of property located at 203

Quadplex

Bowen House

Cedar Street, simply named the Quad Plex. The Quad Plex had been, just a short time earlier, a place where individuals addicted to drugs were living and had constant criminal activity. However, with the renovations – performed mostly by volunteers – the house was made into four independent living apartments, open to recovering individuals and families. Ironically, the house went from a place of suffering to a home of love and support. Additional sober housing beds was made possible with the purchase of Bowen House added in late 2016 and located at 107 Cedar Street.

In December of 2015 there was a groundbreaking ceremony for a new residential dorm. Aspell Manor, located at 331 North Highland Avenue, had become so deteriorated that the expense of rehabilitation and restoration would be

Source: *The Jackson Sun, July 1, 2015*

more financially painstaking than the challenge of replacing it.

A new men's dorm was built on property located at 351

The new *Aspell Manor*, 2015

North Highland through a synergistic financial, advocacy, and spiritual effort. The new dorm has had a positive impact on the waitlist of individuals desperately seeking treatment. The dorm increased capacity by eight beds, bringing the total residential beds for men to twenty. The new building was constructed with energy efficiency in mind, accommodating space for each client, and a common area where the clients could partake in fellowship and attend groups together. The new dorm was made possible, again by the hard work and dedication of Dr. Vicki Lake.

"The community is starting to view addiction in a new perspective. They're realizing that it's treatable – and recovery is possible with the right kind of assistance."

---Richard Barber, interview with *The Jackson Sun*, December/2015

L to R: Jeff Lindvall, Les Jaco, Cornelia Tiller,
Dr. Gus Middleton, Richard Barber, and Dr. Ron Kirkland

Middleton Hall – "The Gus"

As the new dorm was being constructed, the property at 351 North Highland located next door, was being renovated from a three-apartment independent living facility (Tri-Plex) to a multi-functional facility named Middleton Hall; affectionally referred to as *"The Gus,"* after Gus Middleton's support and dedication to the Aspell campus. *The Gus* became the new residential kitchen, therapy group/meeting room, and men residential counselors' offices. On February 23, 2017, a community gathering was orchestrated to officially bless and dedicate the building to Gus Middleton and his family. On February 7, 2021, Gus went to be with the Lord. Gus was an adventurer who loved life and lived it with zest. He was highly respected by all those whose lives he touched personally and professionally. We will be forever grateful for the support and generosity of the Middleton family.

With the new dorm's construction, T.A.M.B. made a bittersweet decision to demolish the old Aspell Manor, and by June, it was replaced with a lush green lot. Today, the empty lot remains a reminder of the numerous lives that were changed there since 1979.

In 2016, The University School of Jackson (USJ) Fine Arts Department presented *"Wake Up,"* a play written by three USJ students to help bring awareness of addiction and break the stigma. USJ reached out to Aspell for insight into how they could write an authentic and compelling story about the

destruction of drug addiction. Richard Barber and board member Greg Stuart shared the positive results of treatment, and the devasting impact of addiction. While the play was not based on any one person's real-life, it did depict the overall adverse effects of addiction and the tragic impact on the individual and the loved ones who struggle to help them. All proceeds from the play benefited Aspell.

In 2014, Tennessee passed the Fetal Assault Law[3], despite warnings that criminalizing pregnant women addicted to drugs would have a tragic and unintended result. The new law created a barrier between pregnant addicted women and seeking medical attention for fear of being arrested on fetal assault charges. While the law was rescinded in 2016, the negative impact remained – pregnant and addicted women continued to avoid seeking treatment and medical attention, including at the time of delivery. However, even for the small percentage that did seek treatment, there were not enough well-equipped facilities to accommodate pregnant addicts.

Pregnant addicts found themselves jailed even without the use of a fetal assault law; a direct product of being caught up in the cycle of addiction. In some ways, this 'avenue' of incarceration may provide some respite from

---

[3] http://wapp.capitol.tn.gov/apps/Billinfo/default.aspx?BillNumber=SB1391&ga=108

daily use and while she may be released, she cannot abscond from the imprisonment of addiction. Of course, the problem with this 'avenue' is that the women were still pregnant, still addicted, and still not receiving assistance for either. There were few national penal institutions with programs for pregnant and addicted inmates; Tennessee was not one. Once in the criminal justice system, the pregnant addict would be escorted to the hospital for delivery and return 24-48 hours later without her newborn, who would end up in the foster care system if no immediate appropriate family could intervene. Consequently, mom and baby were losing crucial bonding time.

> *"Addiction is a public health problem. We cannot build enough jails. We can't build enough prisons to treat what is a public health problem."*
> ---Richard Barber, 2017 Jackson Sun interview

Aspell was chosen in 2017 to directly address pregnancy and addiction through the implementation, design, and delivery of a program called *"A Mother's Love"* (AML). AML was the result of a partnership between West Tennessee Healthcare, Ayers Children Center, and Aspell. AML

opened as an opioid addiction residency program for

pregnant women at the Humboldt Medical Center in Humboldt, Tennessee. AML provided safe detox, residential treatment and most importantly a place where babies can be born clean and remain with their mother. After residential treatment, the client receives community wrap-around services for her, her newborn, and any other children that might be in her custody at discharge.

> *"With pregnant women, you are treating two patients – the mother and the baby – so it (AML) is extremely important."*
> – Dr. Lisa Piercy, T.A.M.B. Board Member at the time

The Jackson Sun covered the ribbon-cutting ceremony at *A Mother's Love* and titled the article, *"A Labor of Love Arrives."* From Aspell's beginning, Charlie Gay, Sr. said the work of Aspell is a labor of love. *The Jackson Sun* article touched on that type of laborious love for pregnant women who have come through

Source: *The Jackson Sun*, September 7, 2017

the doors of *A Mother's Love*. It takes a village of dedicated laborers to see her through this arduous struggle. Aspell's founders would be proud of the work T.A.M.B. has done to bring services to women and now pregnant women.

To date, there has only been one baby that needed to go to the Neonatal Intensive Care Unit (NICU), meaning virtually all the babies have been born clean. A Neonatal Abstinence Syndrome (NAS) newborn hospital stay of twenty days can have an average cost between $13,000 and $15,000 versus a healthy newborn visit of 24-48 hours with a charge of around $1,000. A Mother's Love is fiscally making communities better, but most importantly, it helps babies start on the best foundation possible. That foundation must begin with a newborn's ability to bond with its mother, who is also working on becoming the best mom she can be.

More expansion news came in 2017, with the creation of the Aspell-Hardin County Intensive Outpatient Program. This program was a collaboration between The Darryl Worley Foundation, the Hardin County Healthcare Foundation, and Aspell to

provide addiction treatment. Aspell remains committed to providing the best and most effective treatment services to Hardin County citizens as we do at any other location. We continue to serve as points of light for all who struggle with addiction. Today, Aspell-Hardin county works with up to fourteen men recovering from addiction at the 90-day program. More capacity is being planned for the Aspell-Hardin County program, including pursuing opportunities to serve women in that area.

> *"When you see the light come on in their eyes, you know they're getting it. We give them the tools, it's up to them to do the work."*
> Jamie Long, Aspell-Hardin County IOP Administrative Assistant,
> *The Courier*, October 22, 2020

Aspell has always been mindful of the community's trust. It is imperative that we engage in community functions that make life better for all, whether we directly benefit or not. When the mental health organizations teamed up with Madison County criminal justice systems, T.A.M.B. was eager to be a part of it. In the fall of 2017, the Madison County Commission approved a facility for substance abuse and mental health recovery as part of the new jail's construction.

With somewhere around forty percent of inmates suffering from a substance abuse disorder, the new collaboration and facility would help alleviate overcrowding by assessing inmates for behavioral health issues, including addiction, and referring those inmates to community programs. Subsequently, during trial, it will be easier to divert those individuals, particularly non-violent drug, and alcohol offenders, to a community program instead of incarceration.

> *"Getting people in the program early will get them more entrenched into a program before being released, which would make them more likely to stick with the program and not revert back to their abuse."*
> Jimmy Harris, Madison County Mayor, interview with *The Jackson Sun*, September 19, 2017

Prisoner health is a costly endeavor for the criminal justice system, and once an individual is in custody, the system is responsible for the person no matter what the problem is. Thus, when a person comes into jail, administrators must work with them and start providing treatment. With the new facility, along with fresh medical and behavioral health staff, there are new approaches in creating a custom-tailored treatment plan for each inmate to ensure their overall needs are met. The collaboration between mental health and the criminal justice system has worked well since 2017. Today, more than 100 individuals have been diverted from jail to Aspell alone.

An important factor for support is the ability to show a program's viability and one way to do that is through producing credible outcome reports. T.A.M.B.'s leadership has been conducting outcomes for clients since 1988. However, it was not until January of 1990 that an official and universal outcome study was conducted by the University of Memphis (UM). UM created an instrument whereby clients were interviewed six-months post-discharge. The interviews included questions about housing, employment, abstinence, and treatment benefits. The device designed by UM was called *Tennessee Outcomes for Alcohol and Drug Services* (TOADS), and Aspell received its first results on July 30, 1990: 63% were sober, 43% were employed, and only 8% were re-arrested.

The TOADS program ran until 2008, leaving many treatment centers like Aspell to implement outcome tools for themselves. The following year, Aspell replicated the TOADS instrument, which consisted of calling all clients who completed residential treatment in January (for July-December completions) and again in July (for January to June completions). For a while, the results appeared to produce sufficient results, but T.A.M.B. leadership felt it could be better generated.

In 2018, leadership began reviewing the outcome structure and found it could substantially be improved to generate statistically and more effective data-driven, client-centered, sound results. The *Outcome Monitoring System* (OMS) was developed that improved the six-month outcome reporting with enhanced accuracy and began to capture essential client demographics and substance abuse data points. The ability to track the success of a program is vital to treatment improvements, to apply for and receive funding, to educate the community on the effectiveness of treatment and the overall benefits of an individual returning to society, clean, and sober.

In the most current outcome results (FY19-20), Aspell had a 67% residential treatment completion rate. However, success is more than a program completion certificate. Success is a person who is productive, socially adept, and spiritually sound, living free of drugs and alcohol. Much of these factors are trackable: employment, housing stability, arrest-free, treatment benefits, and abstinence. If these benchmarks are achieved, it gives credibility to less trackable success components, such as establishing (or often re-establishing) healthy relationships, a person's love for themselves and others, and their faith in a power greater than themselves.

L to R: Rick Lutrell, Spencer Cole, Truman Masters, and Richard Barber

On April 15, 2018, Aspell and the recovery community lost a great man, Truman G. Masters. Truman started working for Aspell in 1995 and retired in 2016. We were grateful that Truman could attend the renaming of the sober living house located at 125 Talbot Street to *"Truman's House."* We purchased and renovated the property in 2017.

The huge crowd let us all know; most importantly, we hope it let Truman know, how very much he was appreciated and loved for all he has done for people in recovery. Truman was the most kindhearted rebel you would ever meet. His compassion was amazing. His knowledge about the brain and the disease of

Truman's House in 2018

addiction was exceptional. He could make you sob or laugh hysterically. We can still hear his gravelly voice and infectious laughter today. There will never be another one like him.

"I thought I was just a crazy, worthless man until Truman broke down the disease of addiction to me. Truman broke down the disease in a way I could understand. I was able to recover from drug addiction because I began to see myself as a sick person. Someone able to get well, rather than a worthless person undeserving of love and hope."
Frankie Elliott, Chief Operations Officer, and Aspell Alumni

Truman was known for his electronic gadgets and he would let others help repair them. It was during these minor tech repairs that he was also teaching others to *"keep it simple and stop complicating things."* For Truman, it was just that, because in active addiction nothing was simple and the more, we fought it, the more complicated our lives became. Truman was honest and never had a *"holier than thou"* attitude, because recovery is a group effort, and no one is exempt from relapse.

Life House, residential services for women, was

The new Life House in 2018

operating at 132 Talbot Street until 2018 when we were awarded funding through the Tennessee Creating Homes Initiative (CHI) to construct a new 12-bed facility on a lot we owned located at 127 McCowat Street. The new dorm was completed in 2019 and increased capacity by fifty percent.

Penny Crow dedicated more than ten years to Aspell, working directly with female clients at Life House. She was instrumental in starting the women's program in 2006 and fought for equality of her clients in every way.

L to R: Lindsey Crowder and Penny Crow

Penny Crow died on July 18, 2020, after a long illness, which kept her from seeing the new Life House completed. Penny taught us all how to love women who have spent years feeling unloved and unwanted. She had an amazing way of pushing women to dig deeper and fight harder for their recovery. It was crucial to her that the ladies, after every meal, say three positive affirmations about themselves. Penny always participated saying, *"I am the daughter of the most-high King"* because she believed in the power of God.

There are countless women whose lives are changed because of Penny's sobering glow. Penny gave of herself freely and without hesitation because she believed that women seeking help

Penny's Place

deserved everything. She believed in empowering women to work harder, to make better life choices, and to stand up for themselves. To honor the loving memory of Penny Crow, a house that serves women in early recovery, located at 123 McCowat Street, had been named *"Penny's Place."*

In October of 2018, Aspell embarked upon a new program that would provide additional services to pregnant and postpartum women through the grant Tennessee

Coordinated Response to Pregnant/Postpartum Substance Abuse (TN PPW). The program offers family-based treatment and recovery support services including

outpatient treatment, evidence-based parenting classes, coordinated services for all family members, and wrap-around services that address childcare, education, employment, and income needs. Often clients find it challenging to navigate all the support systems, so the PPW case manager assesses the needs and wants with each client. Thus, both client and case managers coordinate and navigate the system together.

The PPW program works closely with another state program, the Tennessee Family Treatment Court Program. Aspell was contracted by the state in November of 2019 to hire a Family Support Specialists (FSS) to work within the 26th Judicial District Court. During a parent's adjudication in court, the FSS offers appropriate defendants the opportunity to be transferred to the specialized court; however, participation is strictly voluntary. If they agree to participate, services include intensive court supervision, mandatory drug testing, substance abuse/co-occurring mental health treatment services, among other social services.

Jackson Exchange Club honors 2019 "Man of the Year"

Source: WBBJ - https://www.wbbjtv.com/ - June 16, 2020

Every year, the Jackson Exchange Club honors one man who has shown dedication and service to their community with the *"Man of the Year"* award. The 2019 award went to Aspell's Executive Director Richard Barber. Barber has shown tremendous leadership, mentorship, and a fierce dedication to each person who suffers from addiction. A celebration was slightly delayed due to the COVID-19 outbreak but was held in June of 2020. Dating back to the 1940s, the award ceremony is a beautiful affair with the recipient unaware he has won until the ceremony. This year was no different. Aspell was able to bring in Richard's family and friends secretly. The surprised look on his face when his name was called was worth all the secret work that went on behind the scenes to make this event special.

COVID-19 pandemic hit the United States around March of 2020, and the country quickly went into a lockdown. Every state issued stay-at-home orders and mask mandates, meaning that if a person must leave

Source: https://qz.com/1900954/covid-19-is-destroying-addiction-treatment-centers/

their homes, they must wear a mask in public. COVID-19 had a significant impact on those struggling with addiction because of the isolation it created through social distancing. For the addict, peer-to-peer social interaction is often the lifeline in an individual's recovery program. Overdose deaths during the COVID-19 pandemic skyrocketed. It was a scramble for substance abuse treatment centers to maintain recovery social structures while adhering to social distancing mandates. Technology became the vehicle by which clients and sponsors and other recovery support systems could weather the storm.

The financial impact of COVID-19 was devastating to small businesses, and particularly non-profit organizations. There were thousands of nonprofits so financially devastated that closing their doors was the only option. For alcoholics and addicts, this meant seeking treatment would be even more of a challenge. Fortunately for Aspell, passionate leadership would prevail against the financial and social impact of COVID-19.

Since 1979, Aspell's Board of Directors has been proactive, dedicated, and compassionate to the organization's goal to reach the suffering alcoholic, addict, and those with co-occurring disorders. Aspell has faced storms before COVID and will meet them afterward. However, the fact remains that when a cohesive leadership team operates an organization with the guiding light of God first and foremost, it is incredible how organizations can withstand the impact of adverse situations.

While COVID-19 appears to be winding down going into the summer of 2021 with available vaccinations for everyone. The full impact of COVID-19 remains unknown, yet the disease of addiction has an extended history of death and destruction. Addiction was declared a disease by the medical association in the 1950s because addiction exhibits the same components of any other defined disease: discomfort, symptoms, interruptions of daily activities, and if left untreated can be fatal. Yet, today, the disease's etiology remains a mystery, a permanent cure has yet to be developed, and the social stigma continues. Unlike most other diseases, addiction symptoms are often behavioral – theft, violent behavior, suicidal ideations, and attempts – it is the malicious behavior and not the disease that most people judge.

Amid the COVID-19 pandemic, Aspell entered another contract with the state to hire a regional facilitator to leverage resources to create housing opportunities. The TDMHSAS created a second stem to the Creating Homes Initiative (CHI) that had created more than 22,000 housing opportunities for people living with mental illness. CHI-2 would mirror that program for those living in recovery from addiction. Many clients graduating from substance abuse treatment programs burned numerous bridges which made returning to live with family and friends not an option, making housing one of the biggest obstacles they face. Aspell hired a CHI-2 facilitator responsible for going into communities around Region VI to assess housing stock and gaps in housing. TDMHSAS Director of Housing and Homeless Services, Neru Gobin, expressed the importance that any Tennessean lacking safe, affordable, and recovery housing have access to an advocate who is working on their behalf.

> *"Safe and affordable housing is an essential component on a person's journey to recovery, and this investment by Governor Bill Lee and the Tennessee General Assembly will change the trajectory of countless lives to come."*
>
> Marie Williams, TDMHSAS. Commissioner,
> The Courier, January 16, 2020

On November 5, 2020, Aspell was named *"Goodwill's Mission Partner of the Year."* Goodwill has been instrumental in employing our clients in recovery for years. Not just our clients but all citizens of Jackson, Tennessee, who have struggled with employment due to their less than glowing legal and work histories. It is an honor to be recognized as a partner, but the truth is that we are incredibly grateful for what Goodwill does for our clients and the community we serve.

In 2021, McCowat House has undergone demolition, reconstruction, and renaming. McCowat House, located at 119 McCowat Street, first received U.S. Department of

Housing and Urban Development (HUD) funding in 2008 to offer permanent supportive housing (PSH) to single individuals in early recovery. Aspell has received nearly $800,000 in PSH since 2008. PSH funds are used to maintain the property, provide services, and cover a small percentage (≤ 3%) of administrative costs associated with McCowat House and two units at Talbot House.

The newly constructed "McCowat House" has been renamed the *"Kirkland House"* after the generous support by Carl and Alice Kirkland. In addition to the Kirkland's' contribution, Aspell applied for and received a $250,000 grant for construction through the CHI-2 funding. The grant was part of a program that emphasizes matching private funds with state grants. *Kirkland House* is a twelve-bed dorm available to women who have successfully completed treatment and are seeking long-term accommodations. On June 10, 2021, a ribbon cutting ceremony was held celebrating the completion of the building and welcoming of its first residents.

Carl and Alice Kirkland seen cutting the ribbon alongside numerous local and community supporters.

Within the *Kirkland House* project Aspell has expanded the once small and crowded parking lot on Aspell's

Campus. Rather than having a complete drive through campus, we will have separate upper and lower drive through parking lots with additional parking spaces. Creating additional parking space is one of the many steps in a long-term plan to increase our IOP offerings at Aspell, providing greater flexibility for clients according to their work schedules.

"A Mother's Love" (AML) will experience relocation and new construction in 2021. The ground has broken on the corner of Cedar and McCowat Streets to move the Humboldt program to the Jackson Campus. Utilizing CHI-2 and private funding, construction has begun on the new facility, and clients will be moved over within the next six months. Moving AML to the Jackson campus will prove beneficial financially for Aspell and, perhaps, most notably for the clients they serve. Clients will have better access to transportation, community resources and reside on a campus with a long history of recovery-oriented programs, resources, and others living successfully in recovery.

Today, T.A.M.B. has ten licensed counselors, six staff have increased their educational status since being hired, and six have completed education to become a Certified Peer Recovery Specialist (CPRS). In October of 2020, Aspell became a part of the Bureau of Justice Assistance (BJA) Peer Recovery Support Services Mentoring Initiative (PRSS). The program connects projects that are implementing peer recovery support services into criminal justice settings. It also provides a forum to exchange information on promising practices, innovations, and evidence-based implementation strategies.

CHAPTER SIX

THE FUTURE OF T.A.M.B. / ASPELL

Aspell employs more than sixty individuals, with the majority being in recovery from drugs and alcohol. In 2021, Aspell's organizational chart looks quite different than the one from 1979. Our philosophy is to provide every opportunity to make our team better than we found them. By doing this, we ensure individuals employed with Aspell are better equipped for whatever personal or professional endeavors they pursue.

We have more than 271 years of combined service to Aspell and centuries of combined sobriety as well. Those who choose Aspell also choose to serve others, like themselves, to live life free, hopeful, and loving within the serenity of recovery. Each staff member, rather in recovery or not, has commented that their lives have been better professionally and personally since beginning their employment. Among those not in recovery have often credited the Twelve Steps for helping them along their own journey in life.

A new administration is on the horizon to guide T.A.M.B. into innovative and exciting waters; Aspell administration may look different in a few years, but the organization's compassionate and charitable culture will remain the same. Today, we have planted a firm and bright beacon to guide the ever-growing staff to enter those uncharted waters confidently. We are confident that whoever takes the helm after Richard Barber will continue the Aspell culture built on love and family. Additionally, whoever takes over any other position within T.A.M.B. – from Accountant to Counselor to Maintenance, they will have learned from the best.

By 2030, the Board of Directors may be filled with new faces and new ideas; however, they will have learned from the most charitable, compassionate, and dedicated group of folks that have ever volunteered. In 1964, Nancy Tuchfeld noted that the newly formed Board of JACOA was mostly non-alcoholics, serving an organization of individuals dealing with an illness the board member may be unfamiliar with personally. There are hundreds of nonprofits that a person could align themselves with. Addiction treatment is not pretty and continues to experience a debilitating stigma – but these brave and voluntary board members – signed up anyway.

The ray of hope, you see, overcomes the darkness. A mustard seed of faith – today and tomorrow – will be able to move mountains. From Aspell's humble beginnings, through the darkness to the light, and for generations to come, our faith in God's Will and the potential of every client that seeks treatment, has illuminated hope far beyond our beautiful five-acre campus.

> So, Jesus said to them, "Because of your unbelief; for assuredly, I say to you, if you have faith as a mustard seed, you will say to this mountain, 'move from here to there,' and it will move, and nothing will be impossible for you.
>
> Matthew 17:20

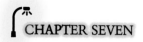

CHAPTER SEVEN

CONCLUSION

As of 2021, there are still only two substance abuse residential treatment facilities to serve the twenty-one counties, outside Shelby, in West Tennessee: Aspell and JACOA. Bob Aspell's presence and influence, his deep devotion to the vulnerable and suffering, and his compassion to ensure others receive the care they need for alcoholism and addiction is the reason these two facilities exist. With JACOA, he had a direct and tangible hand in the building of that organization. However, for T.A.M.B. and Charlie Gay, it was the influence, mentorship, and the intangible character of Bob that built our organization. Because of Bob's lamppost, future generations have continued to light lamps of hope that has made our campus what it is today and will be tomorrow; an ever-glowing beacon of hope.

Financially, Aspell has grown from its humble beginnings in 1979 to its economic challenges in the 1990s, to today with a budget of approximately $3.5 million. Aspell is economically, socially, and most importantly, a spiritually sound operation where clients come first. Our passion and dedication to those who struggle with addiction have not changed in the forty plus years we have been in operation.

No matter where the future takes us, this is a fundamental principle that will never change.

Today's campus is home to more than 150 individuals and families residing in one of sixteen properties located on five acres. The facilities for men and women include programs as residential, intensive outpatient, and aftercare. The campus provides transitional living, affordable housing options, including independent living where individuals and families can enjoy an environment conducive to recovery, filled with supportive services and people.

Clients use the tools acquired from our programs to live their best life, learn how to accept being loved, which caters overwhelmingly to their ability to love others with empathy and compassion for anyone who may be struggling through life. Clients that have completed Aspell programs know what it is like to live in isolated darkness. So, the warm welcome and continued support and love they receive allows them to light their lamppost so others coming behind can see and experience the glow.

This book has covered the organization's tangible expansion, but perhaps the most important and often challenging to describe in words is the intangible development over the years. The development of a client's character, heart, and mind to live life freely and fully, absent of drugs and alcohol.

If the world could extend its compassion like two recovering peers have for each other — our skin color would not appear to have such a stark contrast, the political aisles would not have such a polarized gap, and brotherhood and sisterhood would not just be limited to a church. Aspell is the epitome of inclusion because each person is connected by the disease of addiction and thus can sympathize with the fellow struggler and they can empathize with others who struggle in ways other than addiction. This is what humanity should look like everywhere, not just on Aspell's campus or in other recovery communities.

Nonprofits like T.A.M.B. serve our most vulnerable citizens: our homeless and hungry, the neglected, abused, and addicted, and those living in poverty. These individuals are the weary travelers of life that Bob Aspell spoke about often. Like any other industry, nonprofits cannot survive without the community's support, the charitable giving of individuals who believe in the services, and without the dedicated staff and a volunteer board who are compassionate about the constituents they serve.

Our mission statement reflects our dedication to those who suffer from addiction and co-occurring disorders with a solid commitment to ensuring the community's trust. We would be remiss to end without saying a heartfelt thank you to everyone who has committed their time, energy, and resources to ensure our nonprofit meets its mission. It is evident that many of you believe those who need love the most sometimes appear to deserve it the least; each of you are as dedicated to loving the patient and disliking the disease as we are.

The individuals and organizations mentioned in this book are not a comprehensive list of all the supporters that have given tirelessly and generously in every humanly possible way to make T.A.M.B. the organization that is today. We will forever be grateful to the citizens and leadership of Jackson, Tennessee, as Bob Aspell had been during his time here, for being more than just where our organization is located, but for providing a home for us, in every sense of the word.

For more information about T.A.M.B./Aspell

Please visit our website

www.aspellrecovery.com